The Junior Golf Book

THE JUNIOR GOLF BOOK

By Larry Hayes with Rhonda Glenn

Drawings by David Deal

St. Martin's Press
New York

Editor: George Witte
Copyedited by Carla Sommerstein
Design by Circa 86

Library of Congress Cataloging-in-Publication Data

Hayes, Larry.
    The junior golf book / Larry Hayes with Rhonda Glenn.
       p.   cm.
    ISBN 0-312-10485-5
    1. Golf for children—Study and teaching.   I. Glenn, Rhonda.
  II. Title.
    GV966.3.H39   1994
    796.352′071—dc20   93-34879
                                                                CIP

First edition: January 1994
10 9 8 7 6 5 4 3 2 1

Books are available in quantity for promotional or premium use. Write to Director of Special Sales, St. Martin's Press, 175 Fifth Avenue, New York, N.Y. 10010, for information on discounts and terms, or call toll-free (800) 221-7945. In New York, call (212) 674-5151 (ext. 645).

For my father, Dr. Larry Hayes, Sr.

Who raised four sons on the golf course,
giving us the opportunity to play and
love the game.

Contents

An Introduction to Golf

Golf sounds simple. With a club, you hit a small white ball over green grass, until you put the ball into a specific hole.

The number of strokes used to complete that task is your score for the hole. At the end of a round—18 holes in all—your score for each hole, totalled, is your score for the round. The player with the lowest score wins.

But golf isn't that simple. If it were, the game would be a huge bore and no one would play. Fortunately, the game thrives because it's so challenging and the seemingly easy task of getting the ball into the hole is so difficult. Good golf demands patience, practice, and skill. That's why the game has fascinated millions of people for centuries.

Luckily for juniors, experts agree that golf is more easily learned at an early age. Some of history's greatest champions began playing as children. For example, Bobby Jones, the only player to win the U.S. Amateur, U.S. Open, British Amateur, and British Open in the same year, began playing when he was five years old.

If you're an older junior golfer, however, you still have plenty of time to become a good player. U.S. Open and PGA Champion Larry Nelson didn't begin playing until he was 21, and learned most of his early golf from a book.

The chart on the following page shows the ages at which several great golfers took up the game:

Bobby Jones—age 5
Nancy Lopez—age 8
Lee Trevino—age 8
Jack Nicklaus—age 10
Mickey Wright—age 11
Greg Norman—age 15
Kathy Whitworth—age 15
Larry Nelson—age 21
Babe Zaharias—age 21

Two great champions, Nancy Lopez and Jack Nicklaus, were very young when they began learning to play golf.

Golf is a game you'll enjoy for the rest of your life.

No one ever truly masters golf. Even great champions are always trying to improve, but that's part of golf's appeal.

There are numerous reasons to learn to play. Golf provides an opportunity to spend time in some of nature's loveliest settings with people you enjoy. Traditionally, golfers observe honor and sportsmanship. Golf is the only game in which you are your own umpire and referee. If you accidentally break a rule, you call the penalty on yourself. Golfers strive to be courteous to other players and to observe good sportsmanship.

In this book, you'll learn how to play the basic shots. If you're an advanced junior, you'll gain a better understanding of the golf swing and learn new shots. You'll be reading about golf etiquette, and you'll find a simple guide to golf's rules.

In the end, if you become a golfer who eventually plays well enough to enjoy the game, then a lifetime of fun is ahead.

The Golf Course

When you arrive at the golf course, it's helpful to know the words associated with the course itself.

If you're planning to play, ask in the golf shop about rules and regulations. Juniors may be restricted to certain tee times. Most courses are crowded and you'll be asked to either bring your own group of players (no more than four in one group), or you'll be paired with a group.

See the accompanying illustration of a typical golf hole. The first area you'll encounter is the teeing area, or tee. It's always marked by several sets of tee markers. The tee markers on each side of the tee are sometimes of various colors. Tee markers are designed for players of different skill levels. The back tee markers, which mark the course at its longest yardage, are for very skilled players and professionals. The middle tee markers, which mark the course at medium length, are for players of average ability, such as men, skilled women golfers, and skilled juniors. At first, you'll want to play from the forward tee markers. They mark the shortest course and provide a teeing area for juniors, most women golfers, and some senior golfers.

You'll tee your ball between the tee markers. If the forward tees are red markers, you'll tee your ball between or slightly behind the two red markers, never ahead of them.

You'll also see a hole marker, which gives the yardage of the hole from each set of tees. Sometimes there is a small box on a post. It's a ball washer, and you can wash your golf ball in it.

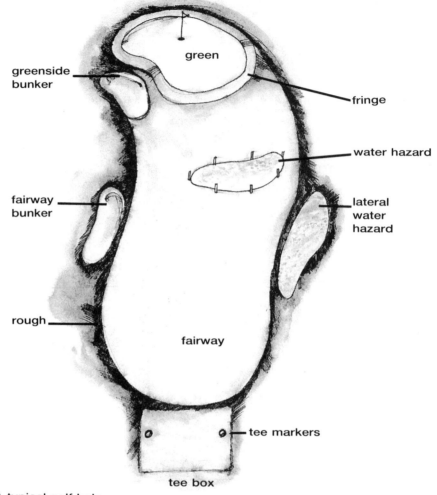

greenside bunker

green

fringe

water hazard

fairway bunker

lateral water hazard

rough

fairway

tee markers

tee box

A typical golf hole

Often there's another small box containing extra scorecards and pencils.

The closely mown area of grass stretching from the tee markers to the green of a hole is the fairway. That's where you're trying to hit your ball. It's a sort of path that is the most direct route to the green and its short grass almost guarantees that your ball will sit well and give you a clean swing at your next shot.

The rough is the longer grass on each side of the fairway. The longer grass slightly penalizes a wayward shot by making your next shot more difficult to hit.

Sometimes you'll see large patches of sand between the tee and the green. These are fairway bunkers.

Most modern courses also have yardage markers between the tee and the green. They can be plaques in the fairway and are often of different colors, such as red, white, and blue. They may be colored poles to the side of the fairway. The plaques or poles mark the distance to the green and they're called yardage markers. On your scorecard you'll find information as to what color indicates which yardage. Red, for example, may indicate that the marker is 100 yards away from the green. These markers will help you to select an appropriate club for that distance.

Many courses today also have sprinkler heads in the fairway marked with the yardage to the green. These are small, flat metal disks that are level with the surface of the fairway. Numbers on the disk, such as 130, indicate that the disk is 130 yards from the green. They'll also help you to select the appropriate club for the shot.

As you get closer to the green, you may see a pond, creek, or small lake stretching directly across the fairway. This is a water hazard and it's marked with yellow stakes or a yellow line. Later in this book you'll find what to do if your ball goes into a hazard. *The Rules of Golf* also will help you.

If the water runs alongside the fairway or rough, it's usually a lateral hazard, and marked by red stakes or a red line. Your Rule book will tell you what to do if you hit into a lateral hazard.

To the right and/or the left of the fairway, you may see some white posts or white stakes. These are out of bounds markers. Check your Rule book before hitting another shot if you hit your ball out of bounds. Some holes have out of bounds markers beyond the green, as well.

Near the green, the grass may vary in length. It can be of the same length as the grass on the fairway, or it may be longer, like the grass in the rough. The grass around the edge of the green is called the fringe or apron of the green.

You'll often find large patches of sand next to the green. These are greenside bunkers.

The green of each hole is an area of smooth grass surrounding the hole. The grass on these greens is quite tender and you'll want to be sure that you don't place or drag your golf bag on the green. Try not to make any scuff marks or to mark the green's surface with your club. If you accidentally damage the surface, repair it with a golf tee and tamp it down with your putterhead.

In the hole you'll find a flag. Actually, it's a flagstick, and it can be removed. You can see the flagstick from far down the fairway and it guides you to your goal—the hole.

Be Safe on the Golf Course

Golf is a game for everyone—children and adults, men and women, boys and girls—but it calls for grownup conduct. A golf course can be a dangerous place.

Golf balls travel at speeds of up to a hundred miles per hour. Golf clubs are swung with terrific force. Unless you observe a few simple safety rules, you can be seriously injured on a golf course, or you may injure someone else.

If you're a new golfer, you need to study the following safety rules before going to the golf course for the first time. If you're an experienced junior golfer, your parent or golf professional has already given you safety advice. A review, however, will help you remember.

Danger from Clubs and Balls

1. There's no place for horseplay on a golf course. Be aware of other players. Golf clubs and golf balls can cause permanent and serious injuries. Even the short chip shot can cause an injury.
2. Never swing a club just to be swinging. Even on the practice tee, look before you swing, and make sure you are aware of where everyone is. Be sure that no one is near you.
3. On the practice tee, never walk out on the range ahead of other players to retrieve a golf tee; you might be hit by a ball. Tees are not expensive. Just use another one.

4. While playing, always watch your fellow players swing and watch their ball to avoid being hit.
5. Do not stand in front or to the side of other players. Stand to the side and slightly back of the ball. Golfers can accidentally hit a ball straight sideways, but not backward.
6. On the course, never hit until the golfers playing ahead of you are completely out of the way.
7. When the golfers ahead of you leave the green, don't hit until they have walked *beyond* the green. If they have walked off but are still to the side of the green, you could hit them.
8. Never throw a golf club. If you're playing with someone who throws clubs, quit playing with them and tell them why. Throwing clubs is not acceptable behavior.
9. The word *fore* is a warning on the golf course. It means someone has accidentally hit a ball in your direction, and you may be hit. If you hear someone shout, "Fore," immediately turn away from the sound of his or her voice, duck, and cover your head with your hands. Don't try to run.
10. If you have accidentally hit a ball that may hit someone else, immediately shout, "Fore!" as loud as you can.

Lightning Kills

Lightning on the golf course is a killer, a serious threat to your own life. Each year, many golfers die because they are struck by lightning. Pay attention to the weather. A brewing storm can move very fast.

1. If a storm is approaching, leave the course immediately! If you're playing in a tournament, you will not be penalized. Even if you're having your very best round, leave the golf course and seek shelter. Your life depends on it.

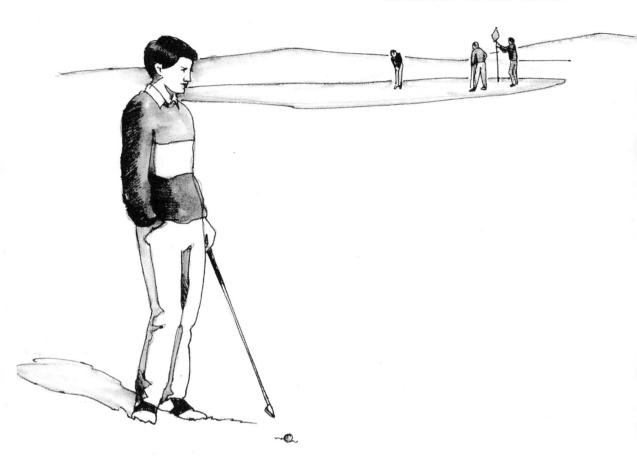

Never hit your shot until the golfers playing ahead are completely out of the way.

2. Never seek shelter under a tree. Trees attract lightning bolts.

3. Do not seek shelter on an open porch, in an open rain shelter, or in a motorized golf cart. You may not get wet, but you will not be protected from lightning. When lightning is near, immediately get to a closed shelter—a clubhouse, pro shop, house, or even a car.

4. Stay away from high ground.

5. If you cannot get to shelter, find a dry ditch and lie in it. Your metal golf clubs will attract lightning, so leave them at least 40 or 50 yards away from you.

Other Natural Hazards

1. Be able to identify poison ivy. It is in many areas of the golf course.
2. Watch for snakes near water hazards, in high grass, in weeded areas, and in wooded areas. If you must find your ball in one of these areas, walk into the area very slowly. Carry a golf club with you, and make plenty of noise as you walk.
3. Sunscreens are newly important. Be sure to apply sunscreen to your face, neck, arms, hands, and legs before you practice or play. Visors and caps give added protection from the sun, and they make it easier to see the ball as they cut out glare.
4. On hot days, drink lots of water as you play to avoid sunstroke or heatstroke.
5. On cooler days, carry an extra sweater or a windbreaker in your golf bag.
6. Watch out for beds of fire ants. One of the Rules of Golf is designed to protect you from dangerous insects, so if your ball, your stance, or your swing will bring you in contact with a fire ant bed, you are allowed to drop away from the bed, no closer to the hole, with no penalty.

The Basics of Junior Golf Equipment

In order to begin learning to play golf, you need access to a practice area and a certain amount of equipment. A limited set of golf clubs, some practice balls, and a pair of tennis shoes are enough to get started.

Golf clubs come in one of four categories: irons, woods, utility clubs, and putters. All clubs have four parts: the grip, the shaft, the clubhead, and the hosel, which connects the club-head to the shaft.

The iron at top has been "soled." The iron at bottom sits with the "toe" of the clubhead off the ground.

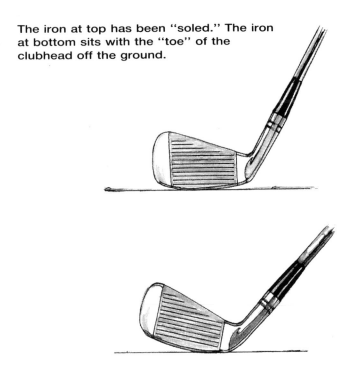

Parts of the clubhead also have names. The flat bottom of the clubhead is the "sole" of the club. A player has "soled" the club when he or she has placed the "sole" of the club flat upon the ground.

Every club except the putter has grooves scored across the front of the clubhead. This part of the clubhead is called the "clubface." It's easy to remember—it's the part of the club that "faces" the hole.

The part of the clubface nearest the shaft is called the "heel" of the club. The part of the clubhead farthest from the shaft on the opposite side is the "toe" of the club. You don't want to hit the ball on the heel or the toe, but in the middle of the clubface.

Types of Clubs

Irons

Irons got their name because they were originally made out of iron. Today they're made of steel or graphite. They're numbered from 1 through 9 and are used to hit a ball from varying distances to a green. Irons are designed to hit a ball a particular distance, not a *maximum* distance. Each iron travels its own distance; they don't all travel the same distance.

The higher the number of the iron, the higher in the air that iron will lift the ball. The 9-iron will hit the highest shot; the 1-iron will hit the lowest shot. Because the clubheads of higher numbered irons are designed to hit the ball high, they will not hit the ball as far. Also, higher numbered irons help you hit with accuracy, because a highly lofted shot will stop within several feet of where it lands, while a lower shot will roll some distance. That's because all the momentum of the swing is used to hit the ball *up* and not *out*.

Players need to learn how far they hit each iron. It will vary from golfer to golfer. There is no set distance you can expect to hit any club. The distance always depends on your own individual golf swing and stature. As you get older, you'll hit each iron farther because you'll get stronger and swing harder.

When you're trying to learn to play golf correctly, find out how far you hit each iron. There are three ways to do this:

On a driving range with yardage markers, follow the flight of your ball with each iron and see where it lands in comparison with the markers.

On a golf course where distances to the green are marked by yardage markers, which are sometimes located on sprinkler heads, you'll learn only by the experience of playing and trying different clubs from varied distances.

In a vacant lot, field, or pasture, older juniors can hit practice balls and pace off the distance to where their ball landed, recording the number of paces. Measure the length of your paces. With a little math, you can convert the paces to yards. If it takes you three paces to walk a distance of two yards, and you hit a 6-iron a distance of 180 paces, then you have hit that 6-iron a distance of 120 yards.

Why do you need to know how far you hit each club? If you know that you regularly hit a 7-iron 100 yards, then when you are 100 yards from the center of a green, you'll select a 7-iron to use for the shot. It's also important to hit the ball solidly so that you hit the iron the same distance each time.

Woods

Woods got their name because their clubheads were traditionally made from wood. Today woods are made out of wood, metal, or graphite. Woods have a much larger and thicker head than irons, and they're designed to hit a ball a long distance.

They also have numbers, usually from 1 to 5. You'll be using a 1-wood (better known as a "driver") or a 3-wood to hit the ball a maximum distance and get it closer to the hole.

Woods also hit the ball different distances. As with irons, the higher the number, the higher and more accurately that wood will hit a ball. The lower the number, the lower and farther that club will hit a ball.

Woods, however, are designed for distance, not accuracy, and knowing exactly how far you hit a wood isn't really very important.

Putters

Putters, described in the chapter on putting (see page 20), are designed to make the ball roll on a green. The face of the putterhead faces almost directly straight ahead, so that the putter will not hit the ball into the air.

A putter with a line atop the putterhead is best for junior golfers.

Putters come in a variety of shapes and materials, any one of which might work for any individual golfer. Juniors, however, will find it a little easier to putt if they use a putter which has a line across the top of the putterhead. That line will help you to align the putter face directly at the hole.

Utility Clubs

Utility clubs are clubs other than the irons, woods, and putters, which are designed for a very specific shot. A sand wedge is a utility club. It looks like an iron, but it's heavier and has a very wide sole, sometimes called a flange, which will bounce off the sand. This is desirable when you're trying to hit out of a bunker. If a sand wedge had a narrow sole, the club would simply dig down into the sand and fail to extricate the ball from the bunker. This is explained in detail in the section on playing from bunkers (see page 65).

Utility clubs include a variety of clubs designed to be used only out of the rough (the taller grass on either side of the mown fairway). They have all sorts of brand names, such as Bafflers, Gintys, etc., but they are of little use to the beginner, or to the expert. Hopefully, you'll want to learn how to hit out of rough using one of the clubs from a standard set. That skill will serve you well throughout your years in golf. The rules permit you to carry only 14 clubs. Why sacrifice a club used for a variety of shots for a club that can be used only out of the rough?

Club Shafts

Another term which might be helpful is the "flex" of clubshafts. If you have a fishing rod, you know something about flex—it's the "whippiness" of that rod when you wiggle it by moving your hands and wrists. A golf club shaft also has whippiness, though it's not as visible as that of a fishing rod.

As you swing, the shaft of the golf club will bend backward, then kick or flex forward a little bit. That flex gives the golfer a bit more yardage. The more kick (or whip or flex) in the shaft, the more yardage you'll get.

If your club shaft has too much flex, you'll lose accuracy. On the other hand, if the shaft has no flex, you could hit the ball really straight but not very far.

The point of matching the shaft flex to your golf swing is to get a shaft flex that gives you optimum flex and distance, but still allows you to hit the ball straight.

When you're young, you need a flexible shaft to help you hit the ball farther. As you get older, because you're stronger, you'll need stiffer and stiffer shaft flexes in order to hit the ball with control.

Some sets of junior clubs today have an extremely flexible shaft, called a "junior" flex. As you get stronger, and move into ladies' flexes, you can use a very whippy ladies' flex or a regular ladies' flex shaft. When you get into the men's flexes, the whippiest shaft is called a senior flex (which your grandfather might use, if he plays golf), followed by a regular flex, and a stiff flex.

Getting Equipped

The high cost of equipment can make golf a very expensive game, but golf needn't be costly for junior golfers.

The PGA of America is a primary golf organization in the United States, and it has a "Clubs for Kids" program in which they take lost golf clubs, cut them down, regrip them, change the lie, and donate them to junior golfers. Most lost clubs, however, are men's clubs, when lighter weight ladies' clubs are more suitable for juniors.

While several golf equipment companies make extremely good junior clubs, appropriate for different age groups, new golfers and very young juniors can use cut-down adult clubs. In fact, I recommend that children under the age of six use cut-down adult clubs.

Ages Two to Five

As a beginner, the pre-six golfer needs two clubs: an iron, preferably a 7-iron, and a putter. As the pre-six player advances, other clubs can be added to the set.

Parents with the ability can make these first clubs. Otherwise, a golf professional or club repair specialist will make the clubs at a very reasonable cost.

Try to find a used ladies' 7-iron. It's crucial that junior golfers have lightweight clubs and ladies' clubs are lighter than men's clubs. If a ladies' 7-iron can't be found, a men's 7-iron can be made lighter by drilling weight out of the clubhead.

Cut the club shaft so that a very short club remains, one which is of an appropriate length for the child. Wrap a leather grip on the cut-off club. The grip should be tightly wrapped, as small in diameter as possible. Standard rubber grips or composite grips are much too large for small hands.

The putter should be shortened and regripped in the same manner.

Most golf shops or pro shops have a "lie and loft" machine, which is used to adjust the horizontal (the lie) and the vertical (the loft) angle of the clubhead. If your golf shop doesn't have one, a club repair shop will. Have the lie of the 7-iron and putter flattened. This is important. Adult clubs are much too upright for juniors, and the toe of the clubhead sticks up in the air. This gives juniors only a small area of clubface with which to hit a ball, and they'll be frustrated by their lack of success.

Before they reach the age of six, we really just want children to have a club they can hold and swing in any way they want. A 7-iron has enough loft so that they can possibly hit a ball into the air.

Ages Six to Ten

Of course, these age groups also depend on size and stature, but the six- to ten-year-old is generally ready for longer clubs and a more complete set. You can buy a good first set, which usually includes a 3-wood, a 5-iron, a 7-iron, a 9-iron, a pitching wedge, and a putter.

At this age, I recommend that junior golfers carry a sand wedge, rather than a pitching wedge, so that they can hit bunker shots. Six clubs are about all a junior in this age group can carry in a light bag, so the sand wedge should be substituted for the pitching wedge. The junior player can use a 9-iron for normal pitching wedge shots, but there's no substitute for a sand wedge. Its unique construction makes it the only club to use from bunkers.

If parents want to cut down adult clubs for juniors, that's fine. This age group also needs ladies' clubs for their lighter weight. Cut the shaft to an appropriate length for the child, and add a wrapped leather grip, wound as tightly as possible. Be sure to have your golf professional or club repair specialist adjust the club to have a flatter lie.

Ages Eleven to Fourteen

The older junior is ready for an expanded set of clubs. This second set needs an added iron and an added wood. A good set would be a driver, a 3-wood or a 4-wood, a 3-iron, a 5-iron, a 7-iron, a 9-iron, a sand wedge, and a putter.

Another good set would be a driver, a 3-wood or a 4-wood, with a 4-iron, a 6-iron, an 8-iron, a pitching wedge, a sand wedge, and a putter.

Children in this age group can also use cut-down adult clubs, but they should be ladies' clubs with tightly wrapped leather grips and flattened lies.

Larger or stronger juniors in this age group can use standard length ladies' clubs, but be sure the lie of the club is appropriate, as well as the size of the grips.

Ages Fifteen and Older

This age group is usually ready for a full set of clubs. Junior boys will not need men's clubs until they reach that stage of growth in which they develop their muscles. Junior girls, unless they are quite strong, can continue to use ladies' clubs. Larger, stronger girls may need lightweight men's clubs. Ask your golf professional to watch you hit some practice balls to help with this decision.

Putters for All Ages

For juniors, buy or cut down a putter which has a line that runs across the top of the putterhead. The line helps with alignment and makes it easier to judge if the putter blade is square. If you can find a putter with multiple lines on it, even better.

Golf Balls

Golf balls are made with varying "compressions." The compression, usually given the numbers 80, 90, or 100, describes the amount of force needed to compress the ball and make it go its maximum distance. An 80-compression ball needs less force than a 90-compression ball, and so on. But 80-compression balls, ideal for most juniors, are generally manufactured for women and have feminine names. Woe to the parent who asks a son to play with a "Flying Femme Fatale"! The best bet for most juniors, then, is the 90-compression ball. Avoid buying 100-compression golf balls.

Used 90-compression golf balls are very easy to get. They can even be found in some grocery stores and are great for junior players. In fact, a used, *top-of-the-line* ball is much better than a brand-new, *second-line* golf ball.

It's best if juniors use a Surlyn or hardcovered ball. It's harder to cut and will last longer. Solid balls, the one-piece balls, are also harder to cut and probably fly a little farther.

Golf Bags

Junior golfers need small canvas golf bags, large enough to hold their clubs, but light enough to carry. As your equipment costs add up, you may want to ask your golf professional if he has any old golf bags suitable for juniors. Adult golfers are very generous about donating equipment to juniors and your pro will probably be able to locate a good used bag for you.

Golf Clothing

All you'll need in the way of golf clothing is regular sports clothes and perhaps a visor or cap to keep from getting sunburned. Most golf courses don't allow jeans, short shorts, halter tops, or shirts without collars, such as T shirts. Avoid wearing those. You don't need to be a high-fashion golfer. Just wear clean sports clothes that give you some mobility and are appropriate for the weather.

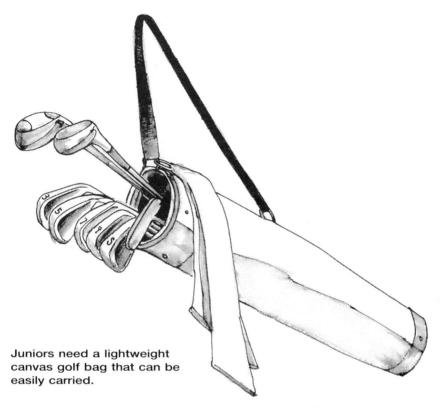

Juniors need a lightweight canvas golf bag that can be easily carried.

Smooth-soled or nearly smooth-soled tennis shoes are just fine for golf. Until juniors become strong enough to at least use full-sized ladies' golf clubs, they don't need golf shoes.

Golf shoes anchor the player a little better. If you have them, fine. If you don't, tennis shoes are more than acceptable until you're 16 or 17 years old.

Be sure to wear tennis or golf shoes. Don't wear baseball or soccer shoes on the golf course. Socks will help prevent blisters.

Golf gloves are not that important when you're first starting. If you're getting blisters on your hands, it's usually because your grip is incorrect. You're probably letting go of the club and regripping a bit during the swing, which creates friction against your hands. A glove isn't going to solve that problem. Band-Aids work fine on blisters. If you can afford a golf glove, fine—but they're expensive and unnecessary.

Lesson 1
Putt the Way You Swing

Putting is almost one half of golf. If you're a beginner, you can learn to be a good putter before you learn the other parts of the game. As you become a better player, putting well becomes even more important. If you become a very good player, you'll make almost half of all your strokes on the greens.

Each hole is assigned a number of strokes—either three, four, or five, depending on the difficulty. That number is called *par*. If you take more than the number of strokes, that's okay: it means you're over par, and that you need to work on your skills. If you finish the hole with fewer than the number, you have done extremely well. For example, the goal of an excellent player is to reach the green of each par three hole in one stroke and hole out in no more than two putts for a par. The expert should reach the green of each par four hole in two strokes and hole out in no more than two putts for a par. On par five holes, the expert should reach the green in three strokes and have two putts for a par. On a par 72 golf course, the ideal round is making 36 shots to the green and 36 putts. Since putting makes up half of your ability to score well, it's extremely important to learn how to putt well now.

All good putters follow a few fundamental rules. When you watch great putters, each may appear to have a different style of putting. Good putters have their own individual stance or posture, but they have a few things in common:

1. They grip the putter gently.
2. Their eyes are directly over the ball.
3. Their back stroke and forward stroke are of the same length.
4. Their bodies stay extremely still during the putting stroke.
5. Their putter finishes toward the hole.

The Grip

When gripping your putter, place your right hand below your left hand, if you're righthanded (the opposite if you're left-handed).

Keep your hands very close together and place your thumbs on top of the putter grip, thumbs pointing down.

Putting is very delicate, so grip the putter rather loosely. If you grip it too tightly, you won't be able to develop a smooth stroke or a feel for distance.

When gripping a putter, your hands should be close together. Place your thumbs on top of the grip, thumbs pointing down.

The Stance

To take your stance, stand up to the ball and bend over slightly. It's important that your eyes are directly over the ball so that you can see the line of your putt, from the ball to the hole.

A friend can help you determine if your eyes are directly over the ball.

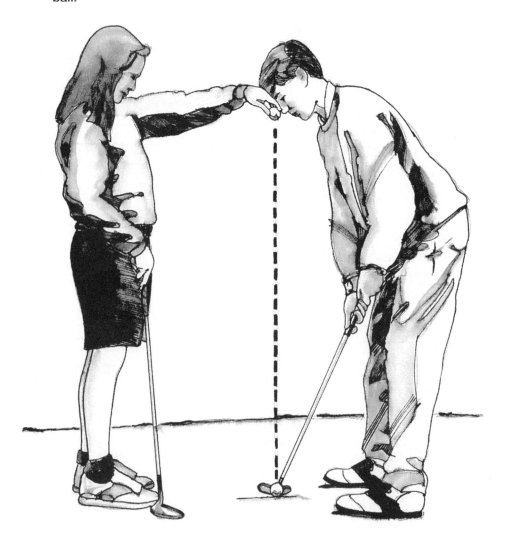

A friend can help you test this with a little experiment on the practice putting green. As you stand over the ball, have your friend hold another ball between your eyes and let it drop. If the ball strikes the ball on the green, then your eyes are in a perfect position, directly over the ball. If the ball hits a spot closer to you, or beyond the ball, your eyes are not directly over the ball and you'll have difficulty seeing your line to the hole.

The Stroke

Now that you have a proper grip and stance, you're ready to make a putting stroke.

In the stroke, the putter moves back and forward. It should move the same distance back as it moves forward. If you take the putter back six inches and forward six inches, then you will stroke the ball the same distance every time.

Try making several three-foot putts by taking the putter six inches back and six inches forward.

What do you have to do to hit your putt ten feet? Try taking the putter back about 12 inches and forward about 12 inches.

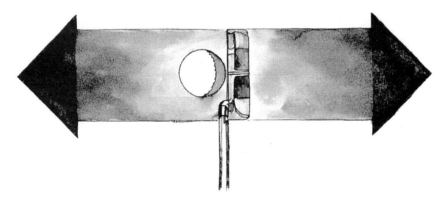

The putter should move the same distance on the back stroke as on the forward stroke.

The length of your back stroke and the length of your forward stroke determine the distance the ball will roll.

In putting, you don't try to get more distance by hitting the ball harder. You get more distance by increasing the length of the back stroke and the forward stroke.

Your putting stroke should be smooth. If you take the putter back too fast or jab at the ball, you won't develop a good feel for distance.

The body should remain still during the putting stroke. Use only your shoulders, arms, and hands to make the stroke. In putting there is no weight shift, so you shouldn't move your body or your feet.

During the stroke you must keep your head still. If the head moves, the whole body moves. Since the putter will move in the direction the body moves, you're going to have trouble putting unless you keep your head and body still.

The Follow-through

A good way to see if you are making a good putting stroke is to check your follow-through. After stroking the ball, hold your follow-through. Look at the head of the putter. Is the putterhead between you and the hole, or is it over to the left or over to the right?

If the putterhead is between you and the hole, then you have made a good stroke and your putter is going back and forward, to the hole.

Practice Tips

- No one can tell you how hard to hit a putt. The only way to learn is through practice.

- Here's a good practice tip for developing a feel for distance. Take a couple of balls to the practice putting green. Place one ball about three feet away from the other ball, and stroke one ball toward the other. Try to stroke the ball just three feet, so it touches the other. Then place the second ball about 12 feet from the first ball. Using the same stroke, try to stroke the first ball exactly 12 feet. Now, again place the two balls three feet apart and stroke the first ball toward the second ball.

- You can vary your practice by trying a sequence of three-foot putts, 12-foot putts, or 40-foot putts. By trying short putts, then long putts, then short putts again, you'll develop your feel.

- Practice is the only way to develop a feel for distance. The more you practice, the better putter you'll become.

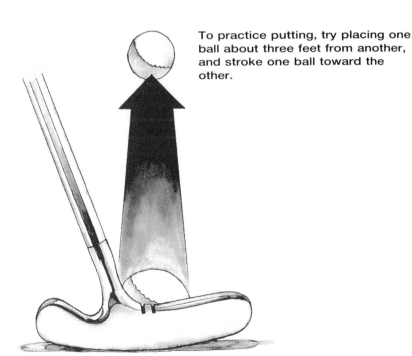

To practice putting, try placing one ball about three feet from another, and stroke one ball toward the other.

Lesson 2
The Chip and Run

The chip and run is a shot you'll use when you're close to the green but not on it. Besides the putt, this is the most accurate shot in the game of golf. The chip and run is a good shot to play when you miss a green and are on the grass nearby. With it, you can get close enough to the hole to have only a short putt remaining. As you become a better player, you'll learn that a chip and run, like a putt, can often be holed. Practice this shot, learn to play it well, and the chip and run will save many strokes.

Let's say you have just hit an iron or fairway wood to the green. You've hit a good shot, but you're not quite on the green. Instead, your ball is in slightly higher grass around the edge of the green. This area is called the "fringe" or "collar."

Sometimes the fringe is cut in two heights. The short, smooth grass surrounding the perimeter of the green can be almost as smooth as the green itself. This is the "first cut" of fringe. There is often another area of slightly higher grass surrounding the first cut. This is the "second cut" of fringe.

If you're in the first or second cut of grass near the green, you should be able to hit your next shot close enough to the hole for a short, easy putt. Some players use a putter from this area. They have confidence that they can roll the ball close to the hole. However, they are putting through at least two, and sometimes three, textures of grass. It's far more reliable and accurate to loft the ball to the edge of the green, then let it roll the rest of the way to the hole.

A television announcer once expressed this well. On the final hole of a televised tournament, a player in contention barely missed the green. The announcer said, "If he's trying to make the shot and win, he'll hit a chip and run. If he's just trying to get his ball close and tie, he will putt it."

The chip and run will save lots of strokes, so let's go to the practice chipping green to learn this shot.

Club Selection

You can use any iron from the fringe, from a 3-iron to a sand wedge. Your club selection will depend upon how far the shot must carry to reach the green and, once it reaches the green,

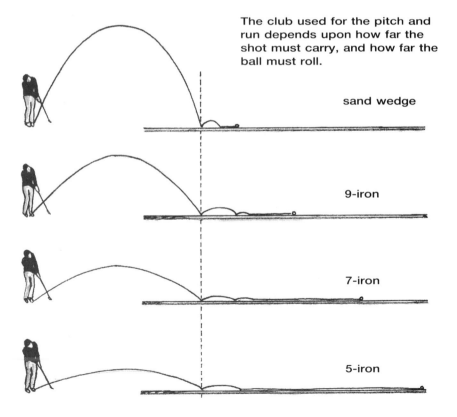

The club used for the pitch and run depends upon how far the shot must carry, and how far the ball must roll.

sand wedge

9-iron

7-iron

5-iron

how far the ball must roll. A basic rule is to select a club that will allow you to land the ball about three feet on the green, and then roll to the hole. From the edge of the green, you can use a 3-iron, which has very little loft. A 3-iron will loft the ball only a short distance, but will allow the ball to roll a long way. As you get farther from the green, you'll use more lofted clubs to land the ball three feet on the green and let it roll to the hole.

Learning the Chip and Run

Only through practice will you learn how far the ball will carry with each club. For your first practice session, use a 5-iron.

Always practice hitting your ball to an uphill target when you're learning a short shot, because you can strike the ball more firmly and make an aggressive stroke. Select a level spot in the fringe, about three feet from the edge of the green with the hole approximately 30 feet on the green, and somewhat above the level of where your ball lies.

The Grip

Grip down on the club, placing your hands just above the point where the grip meets the club shaft. You'll use your standard putting grip. Just as in putting, keep your hands very close together and place your thumbs on top of the grip, thumbs pointing down. Although it's a 5-iron, you'll want the club to *feel* like a putter.

The Stance

Your stance should be much like your putting stance, but slightly open to allow you to see the line to the hole. An "open"

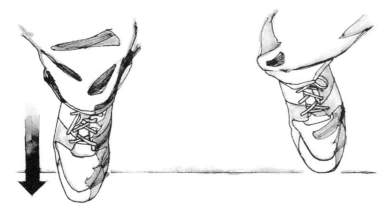

In an open stance, your right foot is closer to the ball than your left.

stance is when your right foot is a bit closer to the ball than your left foot (opposite for lefthanded players). This means your feet are aligned slightly to the left of the target.

Your feet will be fairly close together, with your knees flexed and your weight on the front (or left) foot. To open your stance, move your right foot closer to the path of the stroke, so that you're still over the ball and can better see your line.

Ball Position and Address

Play the ball close to the center of your stance, midway between your left and right foot. Your hands and the grip of the club should be ahead of the ball, that is, closer to your left leg than your right.

The Stroke

As in the putting stroke, use all shoulders in this stroke. Keeping your wrists firm, make a short, smooth, back and forward stroke, like the pendulum of a clock. Try to loft the ball three feet beyond the edge of the green and let it roll to the hole.

The Follow-through

The follow-through tells the story. At the finish, stop and hold your position. Look at the clubface. Is it still between where the ball started and the hole? Is the face still pointed at the hole, as it should be? Remember, the stroke must be smooth. If you're using too much right hand and *pushing*, the face will be aimed to the left of the hole.

Practice Tips

- In order to learn how far each iron will carry and roll, you need to spend a lot of time at the chipping green practicing this shot. This practice will carry through to the rest of your game. Practice can be fun! If you practice alone, see how many times you can chip in. If you're practicing with friends, have each player stand the same distance from the hole and see who can hit the shot closest to the hole.
- In the beginning, always practice this shot uphill. Once you've learned the shot, try it in different practice situations. Move farther from the green. Try downhill and sidehill shots.
- This is a stroke-saving shot. The more you practice the chip and run, the lower your scores will be.

The Full Swing with Irons

Now that you've practiced the fundamentals of putting in lesson one, and the chip and run shot in lesson two, you're ready to go to the practice tee to work on the full swing with the irons. Everything you've learned about the short game will help you in learning the long game—the shots with your irons and woods.

This is ⸻ er long section because you'll be learning the ⸻ ing will also apply to your wood shots.

⸻ iron or 5-iron to the practice tee. These ⸻ learning the full swing; they're lofted ⸻ irly high, yet will hit the ball quite a

```
          TILDEN PARK
          GOLF COURSE
    ....510-848-7373....
              08/12/94

CLASS               31  #
MEN SHOES        44.95  I
CLASS               31  #
MEN SHOES        89.95  I
CLASS               71  #
ACCESSORY        15.95  I
SUBTOTAL        150.85
MDSTAX           12.45

MC-VISA  TL     163.30

     THANK  YOU
#256960 C001 R01 T18:10
```

⸻ e Grip

⸻ nly connection to the golf club. If you ⸻ and use a good swing, you'll hit the ball ⸻ od swing and have a bad grip, you'll hit

⸻ rning, the grip seems complicated. You'll ⸻ res carefully. Once you've learned a good ⸻ b will feel very secure in your hands and ⸻ l become automatic. You need to work

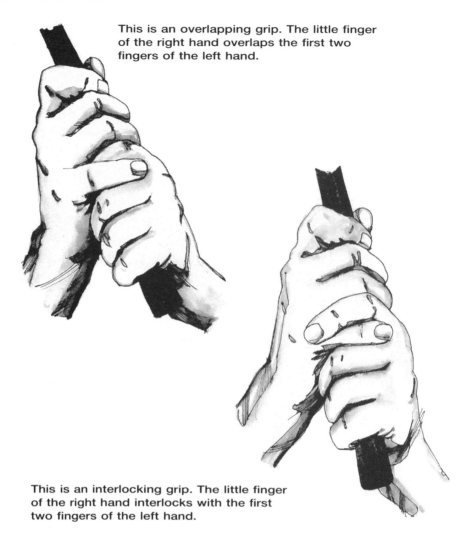

This is an overlapping grip. The little finger of the right hand overlaps the first two fingers of the left hand.

This is an interlocking grip. The little finger of the right hand interlocks with the first two fingers of the left hand.

Almost everyone uses the same grip, with small modifications. There are three to choose from: the overlapping grip, the interlocking grip, and the baseball grip. Older juniors and juniors with larger hands should use the overlapping grip. Juniors with smaller hands will have more success with the interlocking grip. Juniors with very small hands should use the baseball grip.

The Grip with the Left Hand

No matter which grip you use, the entire left hand must be on the club. Your left hand has a muscular pad below your little finger and at the bottom of the palm. Lay the grip of the club up under this pad and across the top inside joint of your forefinger.

If you crook your forefinger around the grip, you can even lift the club by supporting it just with that finger and the pad of the palm.

Close the last three fingers of your left hand around the grip, and the club will be just where it should be. These fingers should grip the club firmly.

The left hand grip is secure when the club is tucked under the muscular pad.

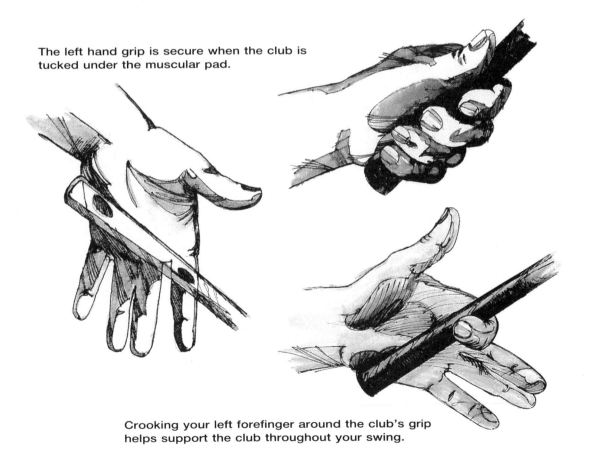

Crooking your left forefinger around the club's grip helps support the club throughout your swing.

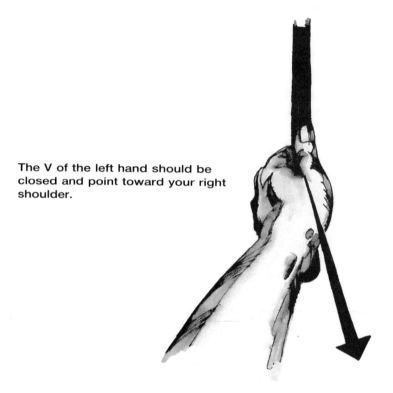

The V of the left hand should be closed and point toward your right shoulder.

Hold the club straight out in front of you with the bottom line of the club pointed at the sky. Your left hand is already on the club properly. As you look at your left hand, the V formed by your thumb and forefinger should be closed. This V should point toward your right shoulder.

Your thumb should be slightly down the grip's right side and you should be able to see two knuckles—the knuckles of your index finger and middle finger—as you look down at your left hand.

The Grip with the Right Hand

In a good grip the club lies more in the palm of the left hand and in the fingers of the right hand.

Now put your right elbow close to your side, and bring your right arm up until parallel to the ground. Rotate your right forearm slightly to the right. This lets the back of your right hand turn down toward the ground a bit.

Relax the right hand until the palm faces the hole, then place the club across your right fingers.

To grip the club with your right hand, bring your right arm up, and rotate your right forearm slightly to the right, as shown below.

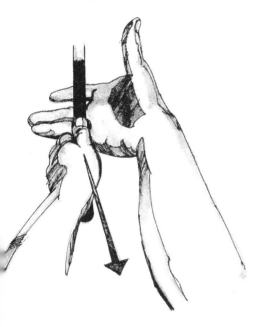

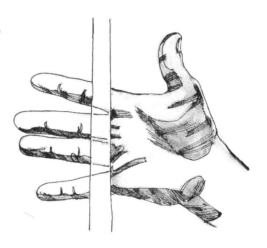

The grip of the club lies across the fingers of the right hand.

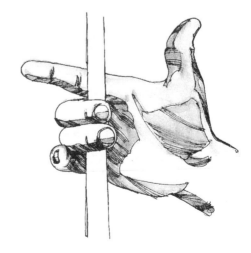

The main pressure points of the right hand, between the first and second knuckles of the middle fingers, help secure the club.

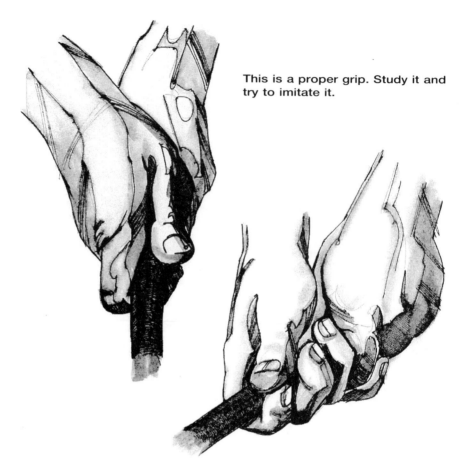

This is a proper grip. Study it and try to imitate it.

A good grip is the foundation of a good golf swing.

The left thumb is covered by the crease of your right palm. Your right thumb lies along the left side of the grip of the club.

The two middle fingers press the right palm against the top of the left thumb. The **V** between your right thumb and forefinger points toward your right shoulder.

The drawings of the grip will give you the right positions. Study them and practice your grip until it becomes automatic. This is something you can do at home.

The Stance and Address Position

Grip the club properly. With the ball in front of you, turn sideways to the target. Stand erect with your feet together, then bend slightly from the hips and slightly flex your knees.

The back of your left hand faces the target. It should hang about six inches out from your left thigh. Your left arm is extended. Your right arm is relaxed.

Look at your left toe, then look at the target. Now move your left foot about four inches directly toward the target.

Look at your right toe, then look at your target. Move your right foot about four inches directly away from the target.

In a good address position, the arms hang naturally, with the hands about six inches from the thigh.

For iron shots, the ball is midway between your two feet in the center of your stance.

Your spine should always be straight, not slouched. Your weight should be in the middle of your feet, and you should feel well-balanced.

Finally, before you start your swing, relax!

Practice Tip

- To check your stance, place a club on the ground in front of you, touching the toes of both feet. If the club points down a line parallel to the line from the ball to the target, your feet are correct.

The Backswing

The backswing means the swing away from the target. To make your backswing, turn the club away from the hole by turning your body. In a good backswing, you'll feel that you are turning your back so that it faces the hole.

As you turn back, be sure your head stays level and doesn't move up or down.

As you turn back, your left shoulder moves under your chin as your club moves away from the hole. Your weight moves to your right foot.

Try to keep your left arm extended.

Remain relaxed.

In golf, the end of your backswing is called "the top of the swing." At the top of your swing, your body, hips, and shoulders are turned away from the hole. That's all there is to it. In this position, your hands will be slightly behind you, with the club pointing parallel to the line from your ball to the target.

At the start of your backswing, turn the club away from the hole by turning your body.

Your head should stay level throughout your backswing.

As you turn, your left shoulder moves under your chin and your weight moves to your right foot.

At the top of your backswing, your body, hips, and shoulders are turned away from the hole.

The Forward Swing

You'll hit the ball with your forward swing. The forward swing happens when you turn your hips and body toward the hole, letting your weight move across to your left foot, and ending in a follow-through position.

In your first sessions on the practice tee, it helps to think, "Turn right, turn left, and finish." Or it may be easier to think, "Turn back, turn forward, and finish."

The follow-through, or finish, is very important. The first thing you're working on is good balance. At the finish, all of your weight is on your left foot. Your stomach, or belt buckle, is facing the target.

You're balanced, not falling down, and still holding the club.

The follow-through tells the story. It can help you learn to correct flaws in your swing.

As the forward swing begins, your hips and upper body turn toward the hole.

Your weight moves across your right foot to your left foot.

If you fall out over your toes on your follow-through, for example, then you're probably beginning your swing off balance. You may be bending over so much that your weight is on your toes.

If your weight falls to your back foot at the finish, you're not keeping your head level during your swing. You may be leaning forward on your backswing, then trying to make your forward swing.

If you're falling toward the hole at the finish, you're probably moving your head away from the hole on your backswing and moving your head dramatically toward the hole on your forward swing.

Hold your finish for good balance.

Swing as hard as you can, *as long as* you are able to have a balanced follow-through and are able to hold it.

Strive for good balance as the club contacts the ball.

At this point, nearly all of your weight has shifted to your left foot.

All of your weight is on your left foot at the finish of your swing, and your body faces the target.

What's a Square Clubface?

To play good golf, you need to pick a target, line up at that target, and swing at that target. This will help you hit a straight shot.

In golf, you always want to "be square." To hit the ball straight it's very important that the clubface is "square." This means that the face of the club is pointed directly at the target, or "square to" the target.

When a clubface is "square," it points directly at the target.

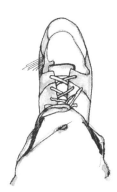

An "open" clubface points to the right of the target.

To check this, look at the bottom line of the clubface. If your feet are on line with your target and you're playing the ball in the center of your stance, then this bottom line of the club should also *point* toward the center of your stance.

If it points at the center of your stance, your clubface is square. You'll have a good chance to hit a straight shot.

If the bottom line of the club points toward your left ankle, the clubface isn't square. It's "open," and facing to the right of the target. You'll probably hit the ball to the right.

A "closed" clubface points to the left of the target.

If the bottom line of the club points toward your right ankle, the clubface isn't square. It's "closed," and facing to the left of the target. You'll probably hit the ball to the left.

If you let the clubhead sit on the ground naturally, the club-face tends to be square. It's designed that way.

Practice Tips

• In your first practice sessions with the irons, tee the ball up about a half inch off the ground. This will help you to hit the ball cleanly and to get it airborne.

- Don't hit more than 60 balls in one practice session. Hitting more will make you too tired to concentrate, so you'll develop bad habits. If you want to continue practice, chip and putt at the practice green.
- Concentrate hard on turning right, turning left, and following through in good balance.
- If you're missing the ball completely, you're probably moving your head up and down. Remember to keep your head level.

At the top of the backswing, the wrists are properly cocked.

If you're missing the ball, you're probably moving your head up and down during the swing. Here, the head has moved down.

- Junior golfers can learn a lot by watching good players practice. Ask your pro to identify the best players. Watch them hit balls and try to mimic their swings. Imitate their rhythm as well.
- If you're a beginner, remember that making contact with the ball is good and hitting the ball into the air is wonderful.
- Golf is the hardest game in the world. It takes much practice and patience. You'll naturally improve the more you practice.

An Iron Session for Advanced Juniors

You're no longer a beginner. You can consistently contact the ball and hit it into the air. This section will help you to be an even better iron player.

As we begin the session, double-check your basic swing: Your head is remaining level on the backswing and forward swing. You're turning back, turning through, and your follow-through is balanced.

We'll next work on a proper wrist break, or wrist cock, which has the same meaning. Remember, the wrists break naturally during the swing.

Begin by taking your stance and address position. With your hands remaining in an address position, bring the club up and in front of you, parallel to the ground. Look at your wrists. Simply put, they are in perfect position. That's a proper wrist break. Without it, you would have trouble getting the ball airborne.

To make this wrist cock a part of your swing, turn away from the hole and then let your wrists break.

Practice Tip

- To check your wrist break and to get the *feel* of a proper wrist break, take your address position. Keeping your hands

in this position, bring the club straight up with the toe pointing at the sky and the shaft parallel to the ground.

Some Advanced Check Points

Be sure that your left arm isn't bending too much on your
backswing. If you have a proper wrist break, you can better
extend your left arm. This creates control and helps you to hit
the ball straight.

Your shoulder turn remains the same—back to the hole, left
shoulder under your chin, hands back *behind* your head.

Your weight should be slightly on the insides of your feet at
address. When you turn back, your weight moves to the inside
of your right foot.

The left heel can be raised slightly at the top of the
backswing, but no more than "a golf ball" off the ground.

At the top of your backswing, look at your left foot. Is your left heel off the ground? The left heel can be a bit off the ground at the top of your swing. If it's more than a golf ball off the ground, you won't be able to return your left heel to the ground in time as you move through the shot.

A good exercise to get proper foot action is to pause at the top of your backswing, and return your left heel to the ground. This will help you learn to transfer your weight from your back foot to your front foot on your forward swing.

Swing as hard as you can, as long as you finish on balance and can hold your finish.

Lesson 4
The Full Swing with Woods

The woods have longer shafts than your irons. The clubhead of a wood, which can be made of wood or metal, is also heavier and thicker than the clubheads of your irons. Woods have nearly straight clubfaces; the front of the clubhead faces nearly straight ahead, causing a lower shot, while the front of the clubhead on an iron faces more skyward, causing a higher trajectory of the ball. All of these qualities help you to hit the ball farther with a wood. You don't have to do anything to power the ball—the club is going to do all the work for you.

The driver's nearly straight face, which makes it difficult to get the ball in the air, means that the ball should be hit from a tee. The driver, or 1-wood, makes the ball fly lower and roll. It's the club that you'll use to hit the longest distance. Golf professionals can sometimes hit a driver from the fairway, but this is a difficult shot.

Your fairway woods, the 3-wood, 4-wood, and 5-wood, are more lofted than a driver and can be used from the fairway or from a tee. Fairway woods can also be used from the rough, but only when the ball is sitting up on the grass, and not when it's nestled down in the grass.

Because fairway woods have more loft, they hit the ball higher, and somewhat shorter, than a driver. They're also very good clubs to use from the tee, especially if you're having trouble hitting your tee shots straight down the fairway.

For your first practice sessions with a wood, use a 5-wood or a 3-wood until you're confident.

The full swing with the woods is very much like the full swing with the irons. A few slight changes will help you to become a good wood player.

The Grip

Let's review your grip. Use the same grip that you used with the irons.

The Grip with the Left Hand

Remember, the entire left hand must be on the club. Lay the grip of the club up under the muscular pad of your palm and across the top inside joint of your forefinger.

Crook your forefinger around the grip.

Close the last three fingers of your left hand around the grip—they should grip the club firmly.

Hold the club straight out in front of you with the bottom line of the club pointing at the sky. As you look at your left hand, the V formed by your thumb and forefinger should be closed. This V should point toward your right shoulder.

Your thumb should be slightly down the grip's right side and you should be able to see two knuckles—the knuckles of your index finger and middle finger.

The Grip with the Right Hand

In a good grip the club lies in the palm of the left hand, but in the fingers of the right hand.

Hold the club out in front of you with your left hand in a proper grip. Put your right elbow close to your side, then bring your right arm up until parallel to the ground. Rotate your right forearm slightly to the right. This lets the back of your right hand turn down toward the ground a bit.

Relax the right hand until the palm faces the hole, then lay the club across your right fingers.

The left thumb is covered by the crease of your right palm. Your right thumb is slightly down the grip's left side.

The two middle fingers press the palm of the right hand against the left thumb. The V between your right thumb and forefinger points toward your right shoulder.

The Stance and Address

Begin by putting the ball on a tee. As you improve, you'll learn to hit your 3-wood and 5-wood from a lie on the ground. Tee the ball so that almost half of it is above the top of the clubhead when you rest the club on the ground.

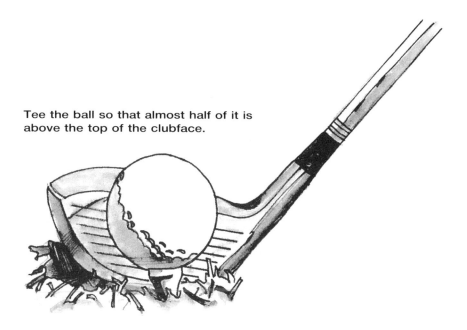

Tee the ball so that almost half of it is above the top of the clubface.

With the ball in front of you, turn sideways to the target and stand with your feet together. Bend slightly from the hips and slightly flex your knees.

Your left arm should hang about six inches out from your left leg. This is very important. New golfers often hold their hands out farther when hitting wood shots. Perhaps that's the mental picture they've formed for using a longer club, but this makes them reach for the ball. It's incorrect, and will make wood shots harder to hit, so be sure not to reach.

To take your stance, move only your *back* foot. Look at your right toe, then look at your target. Move your right foot about 14 to 16 inches away from the target.

When using a wood, take your stance by moving your back foot.

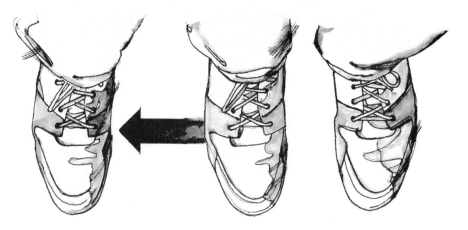

The insides of your feet should be about as far apart as the width of your shoulders.

By taking your stance in this way, you are playing the ball opposite your left heel. Because the ball is farther forward in your stance, don't make the mistake of leaning or tilting toward the target. You still want your weight evenly distributed between both feet and on the insides of your feet.

With the ball in this position, there is a slight tilt to your upper body and your head is a bit behind the ball. That's correct.

Your hands should be about even with the ball, and even with the inside of your left leg.

Remember to relax, and remain relaxed throughout the swing.

The Backswing

Try to make the same kind of backswing you made on your iron shots. The more nearly you are able to *repeat* your swing with every club the better player you'll be.

There is one slight difference between a backswing with a wood and a backswing with the irons. When taking the club back on a wood shot, try to sweep the clubhead back very low and close to the ground. Let the bottom of the clubhead brush the top of the grass as you take the club back.

As with the irons, swing the club away from the hole by turning your body to the right. Try to feel that you are turning your back away from the hole. One good way to visualize this motion is to pretend you are turning to your right to shake hands with someone, using your left hand. When you make this motion, keeping your feet in place, your left shoulder automatically moves under your chin and your weight moves to your right foot. Your left arm is extended.

With a wood, try to sweep the clubhead back very low and close to the ground.

Because the shaft of a wood is a bit longer than that of an iron and the clubhead is larger and heavier, your shoulders will naturally turn a bit farther. This is good.

Remember to keep your knees slightly flexed during the swing and always strive for good balance. Keep your head level during the backswing. Don't let it move up and down.

At the top of the backswing, your body, hips, and shoulders are turned away from the hole.

The Forward Swing

To make your forward swing, let your hips and body turn toward the target. Your weight is shifting to your left foot and you want to try to sweep the ball from the tee.

Finish in a nice, balanced follow-through with all of your weight on your left foot.

At the finish, your stomach faces the target and you're completely balanced.

Playing from the Fairway or Rough

As you grow more confident, try hitting some wood shots without a tee. Use your 3-wood or 5-wood.

It will seem harder to hit a wood from a fairway lie because you must learn to hit *down* on the ball. Woods have a clubhead with a flat bottom, which is called the "sole" of the club. When that bottom hits the ground, the wood bounces back up. Irons have a narrow bottom, or sole. Irons dig down.

As you try some shots from a lie on the turf, make a couple of slight changes.

From a tee, you played the ball just inside your left heel. On a shot from the fairway or rough, play the ball a little more toward the center of your stance—about halfway between the center and the inside of your left heel.

This helps you hit down on the ball a little more. It allows you to hit the ball first, then the ground, which is what you want to do on this shot. You don't have to worry about it. If you make a good turn and a nice, sweeping swing, you'll hit down on the ball. If you try to *lift* the ball into the air, however, you won't strike it as solidly. You'll only top the shot, barely catching a piece of the ball, and it will dribble just a few yards.

When your ball is in a good lie in the fairway, you can easily hit it
with a fairway wood.

Fairway woods—your 3-wood, 4-wood, and 5-wood—are
to use from a good lie on the fairway when you have to hit the
ball a long distance.

You can also use fairway woods from a good lie in the rough.
If the ball is nestled down in the grass, however, use an iron
and you'll hit a much better shot.

Practice Tips

- Hit the ball from a tee at first. As you advance, try some shots from lies on the turf.
- When you tee up the ball, push the tee into the turf deep enough so that about one half of the ball sits above the top of the clubhead.
- Learn to hit woods by practicing with a 3-wood or a 5-wood.
- Remember that a "driver" is not always a 1-wood, it's the wood you hit *best* from the tee. If you're good at hitting 3-wood shots from a tee, but not your 1-wood, use the 3-wood to tee off as you play.
- With woods, try to make a bit more of a sweeping swing than with irons. Otherwise the backswing and forward swing are the same as the iron swing.

Lesson 5
The Pitch Shot

The pitch shot is an important part of your short game. Like the chip and run, it's a good shot for saving strokes.

If you have a large area of green on which to let the ball roll to the hole, the chip and run is your best bet.

For short shots around the green, a club with very little loft (inset) helps the ball run once it hits the green.

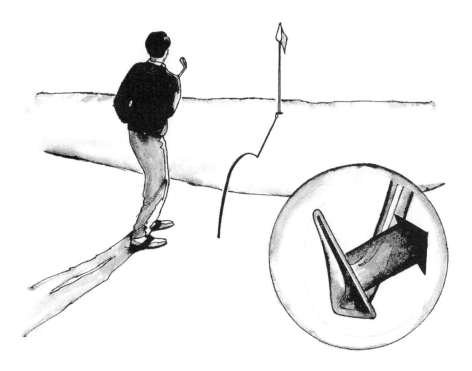

A club with more loft (inset) helps you carry the ball farther onto the green. The ball will stop more quickly, and have little roll.

If you are fairly close to the green and need to hit the ball high and make it stop quickly, you'll use a pitch shot. This is a good shot to hit if you must carry over an obstacle, such as a bunker, and stop the ball quickly. It's also the shot to use when you are anywhere from five yards to 70 yards from the green.

You'll need to practice in order to develop a feel for pitching the ball a variety of distances.

Pace

We'll begin with pace. A smooth swing is important when hitting the pitch. In fact, when teaching my junior golfers how to hit a pitch, I speak very, very slowly. This is to help them remember that the pitch requires a nice, slow rhythm.

As you learn this shot, think of striking the ball with a smooth, slow swing. Let the club do the work.

Club Selection

Generally, you'll use your pitching wedge for this shot. The wedge has the most lofted clubface of any of your irons, which helps you hit the ball higher in the air, from which it will land softly and have little roll. In tall grass, you'll need a sand wedge. The sand wedge is heavier, allowing the club to move more easily through the grass. You may also use your sand wedge for a very short pitch.

The Grip

When hitting a pitch shot, you'll use a regular golf grip—the grip you would use for a full swing.

The Swing

The best way to learn the pitch shot is to take a normal swing with your pitching wedge. Try this in a field where you can pace off the yardages, or at a driving range where yardages are marked. How far did you hit the ball? With a full swing, you may hit a pitching wedge a distance of 60 to 100 yards but, as an example, I'll say you might hit a full pitching wedge about 80 yards.

If your ball is 70 yards from the hole, your normal pitching wedge shot would fly too far, so you must cut down the distance you hit the shot.

The first way to decrease distance is to grip down on the club about one and a half inches and take a normal swing. By gripping down on the club, you have decreased the length of the club. This decreases the length of your backswing and the ball will fly a shorter distance.

To shorten the distance a shot flies, narrow your stance a bit more than normal.

What if you are 50 or 60 yards from the hole? You must shorten the pitching wedge shot even further. Again, grip down about one and a half inches, *then* place your feet six to eight inches apart in a stance that is somewhat more narrow than on a full swing. Hit a ball with a normal swing and a good, full finish. Because your stance is more narrow, your turn on your backswing won't be as big. Although you're still making a good shoulder turn, the swing is shorter and you'll hit the ball a shorter distance.

If you are 30 or 40 yards from the hole, you must hit your pitching wedge an even shorter distance. Still gripping down on the club about one and a half inches, narrow your stance even more until your feet are only three or four inches apart.

If your ball is so close to the green and the hole that you don't need power, the next thing to take out of the swing is your weight transfer. Weight transfer creates power, but this is a delicate shot.

You've gripped down on the club; your feet are in a narrow stance. To take the weight transfer out of your swing, simply address the ball with most of your weight on your left foot.

Open your stance slightly by moving your right foot closer to the line of your swing.

On each swing, turn smoothly, accelerate through the ball with a nice, slow rhythm as your turn smoothly to the left, and follow through.

The Finish

As you've made each adjustment, you have shortened your backswing but not your follow-through. A good follow-through means you accelerated the club through the ball at a slower rhythm.

Even on a short pitch, the follow-through tells the story.

- Did your hands finish at least shoulder high?
- At the finish, are your hips and belt buckle facing the hole?
- Is your weight on your front foot?

Your grip at the finish of your swing also tells a story. Did you finish with the same grip with which you started?

If you have tried to *help* the club through, instead of letting the club do the work, then you have probably pushed through the shot with your right hand. Check your grip. If you were pushing with your right hand, you'll see that you have let go of the club with your left hand and there will be a gap between the club and the palm of your left hand.

If you've swung properly, letting the club do the work, you'll finish with the same grip with which you started.

Practice Tips

- Practice longer pitch shots on the driving range and the shorter shots at the pitching green. The short pitch is one shot you can also practice in your backyard.
- If you practice in your yard, pay special attention to golf safety and be careful not to damage the grass, plants, trees, or the windows of your house.
- Try pitching different distances with your pitching wedge. Begin with longer shots. Cut down the distance you hit each shot by:
  - Gripping down on the club.
  - Narrowing your stance.
  - Taking the weight shift out of the shot by keeping your weight on your left side.

Now try pitching different distances with your sand wedge. Again, begin with longer shots, then try shorter shots.

Always check your follow-through:

- Did your hands finish at least shoulder high?
- Are your hips and belt buckle facing the hole?
- Is your weight on your forward foot?
- Did you finish with the same grip with which you started?

Lesson 6
Bunker Play

Playing from Fairway Bunkers

Part of golf's challenge is playing a round well enough to avoid the obstacles the golf architect has included in the design of the course. One of these obstacles is sand. At various points around the course, the architect has placed hollows filled with sand. Some golfers call them "sand traps," but the correct name is "bunker."

Bunker play is completely different from the rest of the game. The new golfer needs patience and practice to become a good bunker player.

Greenside bunkers are scattered around the edge of the green to catch a mishit shot. We'll discuss how to play this shot later in this lesson.

First, let's learn to play a shot from a fairway bunker. Fairway bunkers are stationed in the middle of the fairway or along the side of the fairway to catch wayward shots from the tee. They're usually large and fairly shallow.

The edge of the bunker, where the sand meets the grass, is called the "lip" of the bunker. Some bunkers are deep, with a high lip. Others are shallow, with a low lip.

From a fairway bunker, you must strike the ball cleanly, and your ball must be struck well enough to clear this lip. If your ball hits the lip, it will pop straight up, come down, and stop. Sometimes it stays in the bunker and you're faced with a more

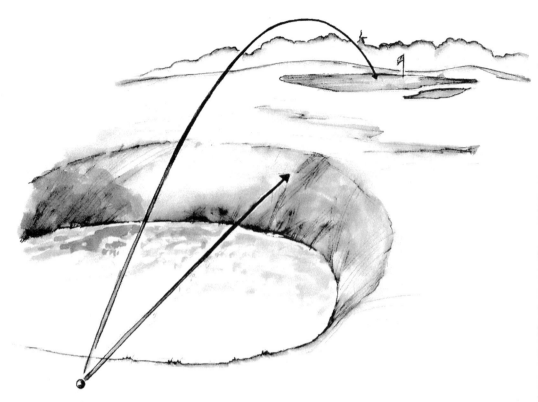

A shot from a fairway bunker must be high enough to carry over the lip of the bunker.

difficult shot. Experience will prove that you don't want your ball to strike the lip of the bunker.

Club Selection

If your ball lands in a fairway bunker, your first decision is to select a club which will carry the ball over the lip of the bunker. If your ball is well back from the bunker's edge, and you have only to carry a low lip, you can choose a lower-lofted club. Try a 3-, 4-, or 5-iron. If you're an advanced golfer, you might experiment with a 4-wood or 5-wood.

In a fairway bunker, we're going to sweep or "pick" the ball cleanly. Because of this, the ball will fly out on a fairly low trajectory.

Because of the way you're going to grip the club, the shot won't fly as far, so select a club one number lower than you would use from the same distance in the fairway. If you would use a 6-iron from the fairway, for example, then use a 5-iron for a shot of the same length from a fairway bunker.

If your ball is near the front of the bunker, or if your shot must carry a high mound or a high lip, you must hit the ball on a higher trajectory. Remember, because you're hitting the ball cleanly, you'll naturally hit this shot lower than you would hit an iron from the fairway, so you'll need to choose a higher lofted club, such as a 7-, 8-, or 9-iron.

Only experience will help you learn which club to use for various fairway bunker shots. Your first job is to get *out* of the bunker, even if you must use a wedge or sand wedge.

The Grip

Take your normal golf grip, but grip down on the club about one inch. This means the ball won't fly quite as far as it would from the fairway, but you'll have more control over the clubhead.

The Stance

It's easy to lose your footing in loose sand, so you must firmly plant your feet. You may want to wiggle your feet a little to make sure they're firmly anchored. Play the ball in your stance just as you would from the fairway. Don't touch the sand behind the ball with your clubhead; it's against the rules. Just hold the clubhead behind the ball and slightly above the sand.

For a firm stance in a bunker, wiggle your feet slightly so that they become anchored in the sand.

The Swing

Try to make a smoother swing than normal. Sweep the clubhead back very low, making sure it doesn't touch the sand. (If you brush the sand with your clubhead on your backswing, you must take one penalty stroke.)

The key to hitting this shot is to make a full, smooth swing while remaining level. Don't allow your head to move up or down during the swing.

On the forward swing, try to pick the ball cleanly from the sand. Finish in a full follow-through.

The shot from the fairway bunker requires a little more concentration than usual.

The Basic Explosion Shot from a Good Lie

When watching good players hit from greenside bunkers, you'll notice the ball flies out in a cloud of sand. That's why the basic bunker shot is called an "explosion" shot.

In an explosion shot, the club never hits the ball. Instead, your clubhead will take a rather large scoop of sand, which forces the ball out and up onto the green. The ball is going to go with the sand.

Generally, the scoop, or "divot," begins about an inch behind the ball and continues six inches in front of the ball. It's between one to two inches deep. Your job is to let the clubhead throw all of that sand onto the green, letting the ball go with it. This takes a fairly substantial swing. Also, because you're not hitting the ball with the club, the ball won't go very far.

The club never hits the ball in an explosion shot. It takes a large scoop of sand, or "divot," and the ball flies out of the bunker with the sand.

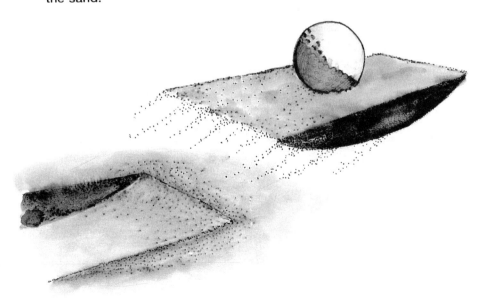

Club Selection

From a greenside bunker, use a sand wedge. A sand wedge has a big, wide bottom on it. It's much thicker on the bottom than other irons. This creates a bounce; the clubhead hits the sand and bounces up into the air. Any other iron clubhead would dig deeply into the sand and stop.

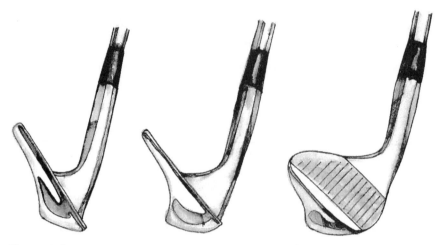

The sand wedge (right) has a thicker base than the other irons.

The Grip

Use your normal golf grip, but before taking your grip, open the clubface slightly so that it points to the right. This will help you to make the correct swing path.

The Stance and Address Position

Your feet and body should aim to the left of the target. Because your clubface is open, the clubface is now aimed directly at the target. This helps you make the correct swing path on your backswing and forward swing.

Plant your feet firmly in the sand, wiggling them until your stance feels solid. Your stance should be slightly more narrow than the width of your shoulders.

In a bunker, your feet and shoulders are aligned to the left of the target, but the clubface is aligned at the target.

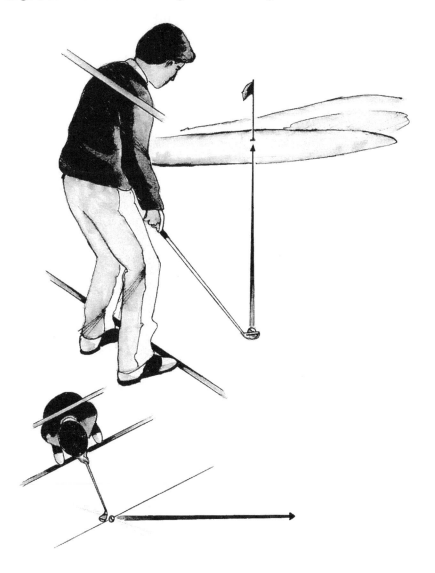

Move your hands slightly more forward and farther down than usual. This lets your wrists break a little more.

Since you'll be hitting the sand and not the ball with the clubhead, look at a spot where you want the clubhead to contact the sand, about one inch behind the ball.

The Swing

Sand wedges are heavier than most clubs and a little harder to swing, so you'll make a large swing to make sure you move the sand wedge as well as you do other clubs.

The swing in the greenside bunker is an up-and-down swing, rather than a sweeping swing.

The path of the swing is the direction in which your body is aligned, not to the hole. The only thing that's going toward the hole is the alignment of your clubface.

On the backswing, use your shoulders to turn your back to the hole and let your wrists break a little more quickly than normal. In other words, the clubhead is moving up faster on the backswing. Make sure you're not trying to take the club back with your arms.

With your eye on the sand about an inch behind the ball, make your forward swing by allowing your hips to turn through and your weight to move to your front foot.

Let the club hit down into the sand and bounce up. The most crucial part of a sand shot is to follow through completely. Don't let the club hit the sand and stop.

In order to throw the sand up onto the green, turn your body completely through. This doesn't mean just to the hole, but through to the point at which your feet are aimed. If your body is aimed to the left of the hole, as it should be, turn your body all the way to the left of the hole on your follow-through.

In the basic explosion shot, turning back and following through completely are very, very important.

Long and Short Bunker Shots

The distance the ball flies is determined by the alignment of your stance.

For a longer shot from a greenside bunker, align your stance just slightly to the left of the hole. The clubhead should be slightly open and aimed at the hole.

Use the same backswing with a quick wrist break, swing back with your shoulders, hit about one inch behind the ball, and follow through.

For a shorter shot, aim your body and stance *farther* to the left of the hole. The clubface must still point at the hole, so you will open it more than usual before taking your grip.

You don't have to swing easier for a short shot. Make the same swing. Since the clubface is more open, the ball will come out higher and will have more backspin, so it will only travel a short distance.

Hitting from a Buried Lie

Sometimes your ball will be partially or almost completely buried in the sand. This is an extremely difficult shot to hit with any accuracy. If your ball is buried in the sand, you just want to get out.

You'll use your normal golf grip, but close the face slightly, so that the clubface aims somewhat to the left, before taking your grip. The closed clubface helps the club dig into the sand.

Line up your body and feet directly at the target as you take your stance. Play the ball slightly back of the center of your stance.

Swing up and down on a path toward the hole. On your backswing, turn back with your shoulders. Make a very aggressive forward swing and try to contact the sand just barely behind the ball. Follow through as best you can.

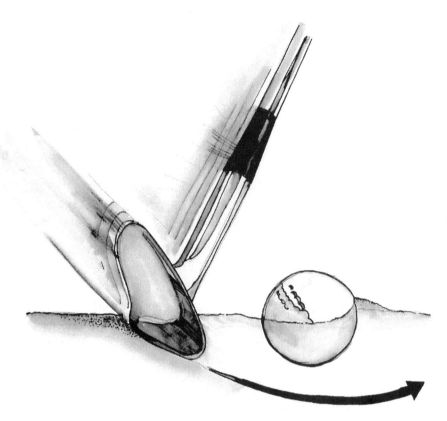

When facing a buried lie in a bunker, close the clubface of your sand wedge. The club will dig into the sand behind the ball, forcing it out of the bunker.

From a buried lie, the ball will come out low and will roll farther than it normally would from such a short distance. The main object is to get out of the bunker. This takes a forceful swing, and it's done with the shoulder turn.

Practice Tips

• Practice is very important if you want to be a good bunker player. Most courses have a practice greenside bunker, but very few have a practice fairway bunker. You'll just have to count on experience during play to help you become a good fairway bunker player. Since fairway bunker shots are much easier than basic explosion shots, you won't have much trouble learning them.

- Use old balls or range balls to practice the basic explosion shot, or observe this tip to really get a good feel for the shot. Don't use a ball at all. Instead use a rock about as big around as a quarter. Put the rock on the sand and practice your technique. Remember to hit the sand, not the rock. The rock will pop up to the hole with the sand. After finishing practice, remember not to leave the rock in the sand or on the practice green.
- Try long bunker shots and short bunker shots. Try hitting practice shots from a buried lie.
- If a rake has been provided, always rake the bunker after you practice.

Lesson 7
Special Shots and Trouble Shots

Advanced junior golfers, those who have played a number of rounds and are able to play fairly well, will notice that golf balls don't always end in a perfect lie on the fairway. Golf courses are full of little bumps, hills, and rough. Often you'll play on a windy day. All of these are special conditions. They're part of the challenge of the game. Without rough or wind or hills, golf would be less interesting.

Hilly lies, rough, and wind also make golf harder, but learning a few tricks will make these shots easier. These special shots help you become a more complete golfer. Golf offers many thrills, such as sinking a long putt or hitting a long drive. Playing a good shot from a difficult position is one of those thrills.

In this lesson we'll offer solutions to these special problems.

Playing from the Rough

The fairway is the smooth, closely mown grass. The rough is the longer grass off the fairway. Rough can be fairly short, only about one inch longer than the fairway, or it can be very severe, grass that is five or six inches long. If your ball lands in the rough, don't panic. There are some easy ways to get out.

A ball that is sitting down in the rough has grass behind it and grass in front of it. As the club meets the ball, the grass will grab the clubhead and slow it down, so you need to make an aggressive swing when you're in the rough.

If the rough is very deep, remember that your first goal is to get back to the fairway. You may have to hit a wedge or a sand wedge—a lofted club which can get the ball up in the air quickly.

If the rough is not quite as deep, you may still have to hit a 7-iron, 6-iron, or 5-iron. These shorter clubs may not give you the distance you need to get to the green, but you will at least get out of trouble and have a chance to hit the green on your next shot.

If about half of the ball is covered with grass, you'll be able to get out, but you should use one club number lower to get the distance you need. For example, if you're making an 8-iron shot to the green and half of the ball is covered with grass, hit a 7-iron, because the grass will grab the club and slow it down, taking some distance off the shot.

When playing from short or long rough, play the ball slightly back in your stance, toward your back foot. This allows the club to come into the ball at a steeper angle, and the clubhead will catch less grass.

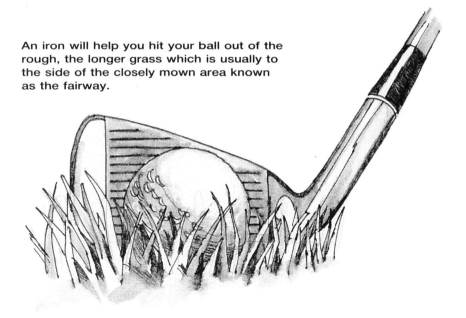

An iron will help you hit your ball out of the rough, the longer grass which is usually to the side of the closely mown area known as the fairway.

On your backswing, make a full shoulder turn. This is a real key to playing out of the rough. You need to make an aggressive swing, but don't try to do it by swinging mostly with your arms. Your shoulder muscles are larger and stronger and a full shoulder turn will give you more power, helping you to get the ball back into play on the fairway, or onto the green.

On your forward swing, hit down and through the ball. In other words, feel as if you're going to make a large divot after striking the ball.

If the rough is quite long, the grass will grab the hosel, the part of the club which connects the clubhead to the shaft. This slows down the heel of the club, but the toe of the clubface keeps going and the clubface is closed when it comes into the ball. This causes the ball to fly to the left. To overcome this, in longer grass you may want to open the clubface slightly before taking your grip.

Remember, your first goal is to get out of the rough. Be sure to use a club with enough loft to get you out.

Hilly Lies

Uphill Lie

If your ball is on an uphill slope, where your left foot is higher than your right, you need to make some adjustments.

The ball will tend to go to the left, so aim slightly right of your target. When you address the ball, make sure that your shoulders are the same slope as the hill. On an uphill lie, you want your left shoulder higher and your right shoulder lower, so that you're not leaning into the slope.

Play the ball slightly forward in your stance. This will give you a more sweeping swing, so that you won't hit into the hillside. If the slope is severe, the ball will be launched rather high. A higher shot won't go as far, so take one club number lower: a 5-iron instead of a 6-iron.

Try to make your usual smooth swing—turn right, turn left, and finish as best you can.

A ball above your feet (see page 80) will tend to go to the left.

Downhill Lie

A ball on a downhill slope, where your right foot is higher than your left, will tend to go to the right, so aim slightly left of your target. If the slope is severe, the club will not have its usual loft when it comes into the ball. The ball will fly lower, so use a more lofted club.

Play the ball slightly back in your stance. Make sure that your shoulders match the slope, with your left shoulder down and your right shoulder up a bit.

Turn right, and turn left. You'll have no trouble following through on this shot.

Ball Above Your Feet

On a hillside, if the ball is above your feet it will fly to the left, so aim a bit to the right of your target.

The ball is closer to your hands than it would be on level ground, so grip down on the club an inch, or so. Because you grip down, the club is now somewhat shorter and the ball may not fly as far. You may want to use a slightly less lofted club than you would use from a level lie. If you would use a 4-iron from a level lie, for example, use a 3-iron when the ball lies above your feet.

On this shot, try to stand a little taller with more erect posture. While you'll easily be able to make a swing, keep your swing smooth and rhythmical, stay level, and make sure you make solid contact.

Ball Below Your Feet

At address, bend from the hips a little more than normal so that you can reach the ball. The ball will tend to go to the right, so aim a bit to the left of your target.

A ball below your feet will tend to go to the right.

It's very important to remain level during this shot. Keep the bend from the hips while you swing; don't rise and return to your normal posture. Swing very smoothly.

Wind Shots

Into the Wind from the Tee

A strong wind will dramatically affect your ball. If you're teeing off into the wind, you'll automatically lose some distance. To lose as little distance as possible, the ball must be hit on a low trajectory, "under" the wind. Tee the ball lower, and play the ball back in the center of your stance. For balance, widen your stance slightly. Since wrists add height in a golf swing, you don't want to be quite as wristy. Your wrists should be firmer during the swing. Don't try to hit the ball harder to compensate for the wind. Swing smoothly. As the great Patty Berg, who won 15 major championships, says, "When it's breezy, swing easy."

Into the Wind from the Fairway

For a shot into the wind, take one extra club—that is, a less-lofted club that will keep the ball lower. If you'd use a 5-iron on a windless day, use a 4-iron when hitting into the wind. Grip down on the club about one inch and stand two inches closer to the ball than normal. Play the ball slightly back in your stance. Addressing the ball with your hands a bit farther in front of the ball will help you to hit it low, but be sure the clubface remains square to the target. On the backswing, keep your hands ahead of the ball until the clubhead is on its way. For balance, your stance should be slightly wider. Swing smoothly.

Downwind from the Tee

Tee the ball at its normal height. Play the ball slightly forward in your stance. Take a normal stance with your hands in their normal position. Make sure you don't swing harder; it's not necessary. Swing slowly and smoothly. You'll be able to take advantage of the wind to get more distance.

Downwind from the Fairway

If you're using an iron, play the ball about two inches farther forward than normal in your stance. Your hands remain in their normal position. This will make you feel that your head is slightly behind the ball—make sure it stays there during the swing. Sweep the club back low. Generally, you'll need a little less club because the wind will move the ball forward. A normal 6-iron shot will now go the distance of a 5-iron, so select your club carefully.

Crosswind

If the wind is blowing hard from your right to your left, aim a bit to the right and let the wind move the ball to the left. Make your normal swing, but always swing smoothly in the wind. If the wind is blowing from your left, aim a bit to the left and let the wind move the ball back to the right. Again, make your normal swing and make sure you swing smoothly.

Practice Tips

- These shots require experience, so that you can learn how various conditions affect your ability to strike the ball. Hilly lies and shots from the rough can usually be experienced only during a round of golf. However, you can practice wind shots on the practice tee even on a calm day, by trying to hit the ball high and low with your driver. Practice the adjustments for wind with your irons.

- A smooth, relaxed swing and good balance are always important. From a hilly lie or on a windy day, they're even more important.
- Wind tends to make most golfers speed up their swings. Remember to swing slowly for better results.

Lesson 8
Playing the Golf Course

Playing golf is very different from practicing.

A good golfer is a complete golfer. A good golfer has a sound swing and can hit the ball a fair distance, but the good golfer also has an accurate short game and is smart on the course.

Golf is a game of strategy. It demands that you use your head. Very often a player who doesn't seem to be a great natural athlete can shoot a lower score than a player with a great swing. And a golfer who has a good short game and plays intelligently can beat a golfer who hits the ball a long way.

In golf, you're on your way to becoming a good player if you learn to always play the shot with which you have the highest probability of success. That's how to lower your scores.

It's important to know how to *play* the golf course. These are proven ways to play a course, methods used by top tournament professionals and amateurs which will also help the junior golfer.

A Tip for Beginners

One of the most important things a new golfer can do is to be sure to hit the ball every time and move it forward. Swinging hard and missing the ball time after time isn't any fun.

Your first goal is to meet the ball solidly and make it go forward. Even if you hit it to the right or to the left, hitting the ball solidly every time should be your biggest priority.

On the Tee

On each tee, don't just aim at the fairway. Pick a specific target. Choose a dark patch of grass on the fairway, a tree in the distance, or a faraway chimney, but pick a specific spot to hit to. If you choose a target which lines up with the fairway and aim at it, even if your ball moves a bit to the right or to the left of that target, you'll have a better chance of hitting the fairway.

When standing on the tee, look down the fairway and see where the trouble is located. Is a grove of trees growing in the right rough? Is there a water hazard on the left? Once you've located the trouble, you'll know which side of the tee to choose for teeing your ball.

If the trouble is on the right, tee your ball on the right side of the teeing area. To hit to the center of the fairway, you'll now be aiming a bit to the left and you'll be hitting *away* from the trouble.

In the same way, if the trouble is on the left, tee your ball on the left side of the tee. You'll now be aiming a bit to the right, in order to hit to the center of the fairway. Again, you'll be hitting away from the trouble.

So always tee up your ball on the same side as the trouble, and you'll be hitting away from it.

Shots from the Fairway and Rough

After your tee shot, you're faced with playing your second shot. Always look at your lie. If your ball is sitting up very nicely in the fairway, if there are no humps or bumps behind the ball, you can hit a wood. If your ball is sitting down in the grass in the fairway, or there's a little hump behind it, or it's in a divot, you'll need to hit an iron.

If you're in the rough, hit an iron instead of a wood. Since it's much easier to solidly contact a ball in high grass with an iron than with a wood, and easier to get the ball airborne, you'll be able to move the ball forward a fair distance without risking a mishit shot. Always use the club that guarantees success, especially in the rough, even if you must use a 9-iron to get back into the fairway.

Hitting out of Trouble

If your ball is in a stand of trees, your first goal is to get the ball back into play. Don't take risks. For example, don't try to chip or hit the ball through a narrow opening. You don't want to waste two or three strokes banging around in the trees.

If possible, you want to get back into play—into the fairway—in one stroke, so pick the widest opening between trees. Get that ball back into play, even if it means going slightly backward.

For now, don't take unnecessary risks by trying to hit over a tree or under a low-hanging limb. Pick an escape route where you can either hit your normal shot or hit a chip shot to get back to the fairway.

Approaching the Green

On an approach shot to the green, play smart. You're trying to minimize risks to save strokes. A good golfer doesn't always aim at the flagstick. If the flagstick is behind a bunker, or if it's on the extreme right or the extreme left side of the green, aim at the middle of the green instead of at the flagstick. There's more room for error.

Good players don't always aim at the flagstick, especially when it's behind a bunker.

When you aim directly at a flagstick located on the extreme right side of the green, if you hit your ball just slightly to the right, you've missed the green.

The same strategy applies if the hole is cut behind a bunker. If you mishit your ball just a bit, not hitting it as far as you would normally hit it, you're in the sand.

Don't always aim at the flagstick. Your priority is to get on the green, where you can make a putt.

Bunkers

If your ball is in a bunker, your goal is to get out and onto the green, not necessarily to hit the ball close to the hole. Always make sure that you hit the shot that will get you out. Sometimes you may even have to play out to the side, if you're in the face of a deep bunker which has a very high lip.

Putting

On the green, your goal is to two-putt. Try to imagine a large barrel around the hole. On your first putt, your job is to make the ball stop inside the imaginary barrel for a short, easy second putt. This requires some thought. Is the putt uphill, or downhill? Does it break to the right, or to the left? On the putting green, if the slope of the ground is to the right, your ball will move or "break" to the right when it rolls across the slope. If the slope is angled to the left, your ball will break or roll to the left. Putt your ball accordingly.

On long putts, try to leave your first putt within an imaginary "barrel" around the hole. You'll have an easy second putt.

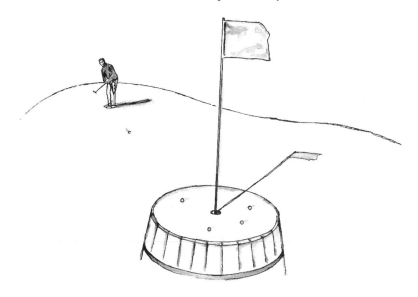

Try to get a feel for how hard you need to stroke your putt, when the ball is going to slow down, and when it slows down where it's going to stop. If you leave the first putt inside that barrel, the second putt is that much easier.

Really concentrate on short putts. They're just as important as long putts. Be sure your putter always finishes toward the hole. Don't play "gimmees," in which you and your friends concede short putts. That's bad practice. You need to consistently see the ball going into the hole, time after time. It builds confidence.

Analyzing Your Game

After completing a hole, try to review the hole you last played. There's not always time for a review. New efforts are under way to speed up the game, and all golfers are expected to immediately go to the next tee and hit their shots. At times, however, such as while you're walking to the next tee or awaiting your turn to hit, you can review your play on the previous hole and analyze your mistakes.

For example, "I wasted a shot because I hit my ball into the trees and tried to take a risk." At the end of a round, analyze problems and where you lost shots. You may decide that your second shots gave you a problem, or your tee shots, or your short game. What was your biggest problem? What shot do you most need to work on? This gives you a goal for your next practice session.

Quite often, you'll discover that you wasted more strokes with your short game.

Keep records. You'll most likely want to do this after a round, but you can keep records during a round if you don't hold up play. Carry an extra scorecard on which to make notes. Next to your score for each hole write down the number of putts you took on that hole.

HOLE	1	2	3	4	5	6	7	8	9	OUT
YARDAGE	500	385	167	514	329	131	359	523	155	3063
JEFF	7	5	3	7	6	4	5	6	4	47
CHAD	5	5	4	6	6	4	6	6	5	47
TAMMY	6	5	4	6	5	3	5	6	4	44
PAR	5	4	3	5	4	3	4	5	3	36
HANDICAP	11	3	5	1	15	17	7	9	13	
JEFF	w- SG			I SG	SG	I		w SG	I	
	3p.	2p.	1p.	3p.	2p.	2p.	2p.	2p.	2p.	

Keep records and devise a code to show which parts of your game need work.

Develop a little code for the shots you missed. For example, write a small "w" if you missed a wood shot, a small "i" for a missed iron shot, or a small "sg" for a missed shot in your short game.

This is how golfers often plan their practice and improve. When you get to this point, you've become a true student of the game.

Some Simple Golf Rules

Golf's rules have an important purpose—to assure that everyone plays the same game and plays it fairly. Learning the rules outlined in this chapter will help you to learn how the game is correctly played.

Golf's basic idea is, on each hole, to play your first shot from the tee, then to strike the ball with a club until you have holed out on the putting green of that hole. The number of strokes with which you accomplish this is your score for the hole. The golf course is divided into 18 holes: the front nine and the back nine. At the end of 18 holes, add your scores for each hole and the total is your score for the round.

Ideally, on each hole you would never touch the ball from the time you place it on a tee until you take it out of the hole. During a round of golf, however, the rules allow you to touch the ball in some situations. We'll review most of these situations and the rest can be found in any copy of *The Rules of Golf*, a booklet which is sold at most golf courses.

Everyone hits a number of imperfect shots during a round. You may hit your ball into a bunker, into a water hazard, or out of bounds. Understanding the rules covering these situations will help you know how to proceed.

Before You Play

Count your golf clubs. You're allowed to carry no more than fourteen.

Put an identifying mark on your ball: a dot from a magic marker, or a pencil mark will do.

Don't ask advice from anyone except your partner or your caddie.

Don't give advice to anyone except your partner.

On the Tee

In an informal game, on the first tee decide among yourselves who's going to tee off first. On following holes, the player who had the lowest score on the previous hole has "the honor," and tees off first. If you all had the same score, the player who hit first on the previous tee goes first.

You may tee your ball as much as two club lengths behind the tee markers, but not ahead of the markers.

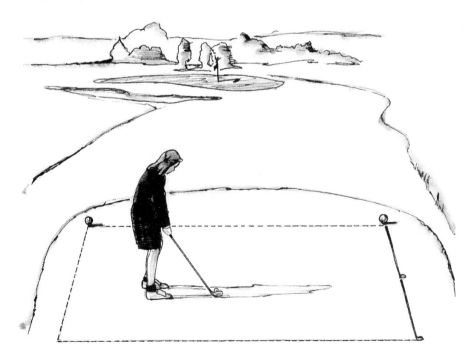

Tee off between the tee markers. You may tee the ball even with the markers or as much as two club lengths behind them, but not ahead of the markers.

If your ball falls off the tee before you swing, there's no penalty and you may replace it. If it falls off the tee when you swing, play the ball where it lies and add a penalty stroke to your score for the hole.

On the Course

The ball farther from the hole is played first, so if you are playing with a friend and your tee shot is longer, your friend hits first.

Play the ball as it lies. Don't touch it unless a rule permits.

If you accidentally move your ball, return it to its original position and add a penalty stroke. If your ball moves when you remove *natural* objects, such as loose grass, sticks, leaves, etc., in an area within one club length of your ball, replace it and add a penalty stroke.

Play the course as you find it. Don't move or break anything growing or imbedded that might interfere with your ball, your stroke, or your line of play.

Hazards

A hazard is any lake, sea, pond, river, or ditch marked by yellow lines or yellow stakes. Hazards usually lie across the fairway. A lateral hazard is any lake, sea, pond, river, or ditch marked by red lines or red stakes. Lateral hazards usually lie to the side of the fairway.

A bunker is also a hazard. Bunkers are hollows from which grass has been removed and replaced with sand. Grass growing around or in the bunker isn't part of the hazard.

If your ball goes into a hazard and you can't play it, drop the ball behind the hazard. You may drop as far behind the hazard as you wish—just keep the spot where your ball last crossed the edge of the hazard between your ball and the hole. Alternatively, you may also replay the shot from where you originally played. In either case, add a penalty stroke to your score for the hole.

If your ball goes into a lateral hazard and can't be played, you may replay the shot from your original position, or you may drop another ball within two club lengths of the spot where your ball last crossed the edge of the hazard, but no closer to the hole.

Or, you may drop a ball on the other side of the lateral hazard. For example, a ditch running the length of the fairway

A lateral hazard. This shows the two places where you are permitted to drop your ball.

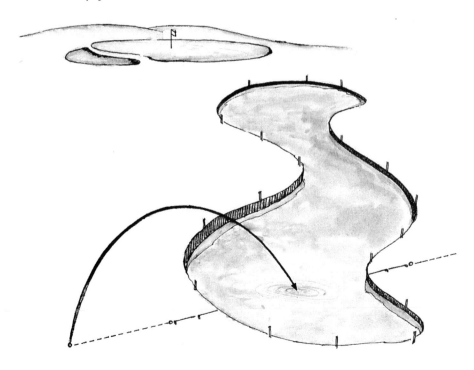

marked by red stakes is a lateral hazard. You could drop your ball to the right, or to the left, of the ditch. The ball must be dropped within two club lengths of a spot that is an equal distance from the hole as the spot where your ball last crossed the edge of the hazard, and no closer to the hole. Add one penalty stroke to your score.

If your ball is in a bunker or a hazard, you may be able to hit it. Be sure to observe these rules: Don't test the condition of the ground or water in any way, whether with your hand, club, foot, etc. Don't ground your club. Don't remove any loose sticks, grass clippings, or rocks, etc., when you're in a hazard. Just step in and play your shot.

Out of Bounds

Out of bounds is usually marked by white stakes or a white line. It's an area of ground on which play is prohibited. Sometimes a fence or wall marks out of bounds, and this is usually noted on the scorecard under "Local Rules."

Your ball is out of bounds when all of the ball lies out of bounds.

If you hit a ball out of bounds, you must play another ball from your original position. At the end of the hole, count all of your strokes, including the strokes you made with your first ball, and add a penalty stroke.

If you think you've hit a ball out of bounds, you may hit a *provisional ball* from the spot where you hit your original ball. If you find your original ball and it's not out of bounds, just pick up the provisional ball and play your original. There's no penalty. If your original ball is out of bounds, the provisional ball is in play. Again, at the end of the hole, you must count all of your strokes, including the original stroke that went out of bounds, and add a penalty stroke.

Lost Ball

A ball is lost if you can't find it and identify it as yours within a five-minute search. If your ball is lost, play another ball from where you hit your original ball. Count your original stroke, all the strokes you made on the hole, and add a penalty stroke.

On the Putting Green

You may remove sand or loose soil from the line of your putt. You may remove natural objects from the line of your putt, such as sticks, stones, or pieces of grass or turf, as long as they're not attached or imbedded. You may remove anything artifical from the line of your putt. Otherwise, never touch the line of your putt, even with the head of your putter.

You may lift your ball to clean it. You must replace it. You may lift your ball if it interferes with another player's putt, then replace it.

When lifting your ball, you must first mark your ball. Do this by placing a small coin or marker behind the ball, then lift your ball. Be sure you return it to its original spot when it's your turn to play.

On the green, mark your ball by placing a small coin or marker behind it.

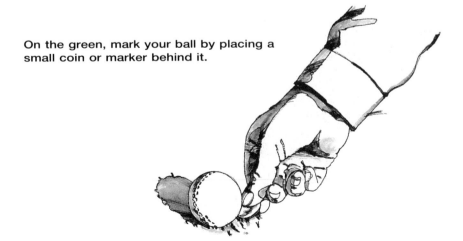

On your line of putt, you may repair damage caused by a ball hitting the green.

You may not repair marks or scuffs caused by golf shoe spikes until everyone in your group has holed out.

When you are on the green, there's a two-stroke penalty if your ball strikes the flagstick. Remove the flagstick before you putt, or have someone "tend the flagstick," holding it until your ball nears the hole, then pulling the flagstick from the hole. There is no penalty if your ball hits the flagstick from a shot taken from off the green.

If your ball is on the green and strikes another player's ball when you putt, you are penalized two strokes. Always ask another player to mark his ball if you think it will interfere with yours.

Always hole out before you leave the green. Golf's rules allow no "gimme" putts in stroke play.

Practice

You may make practice swings anywhere on the golf course except in a hazard, lateral hazard, or bunker. Practice *strokes*, in which you hit a ball for practice, are not allowed.

Scoring

Be sure your score for each hole is accurate. At the end of the round, add your scores for each hole and sign your scorecard. If someone else kept the scorecard, sign on the line marked "attest." If you kept the card, sign on the line marked "scorer," and have one of the other players in your group sign the card on the line marked "attest." This means you both agree that the scores on the card are correct.

When playing in a tournament you must always sign your scorecard, turn in the correct score, and turn in your scorecard promptly.

At the end of your round, always check your scorecard carefully before signing it.

Lesson 10
Golf Etiquette

Golf is a game for ladies and gentleman, no matter how young or how old they may be.

Consideration is a traditional part of the game and makes golf more pleasant for everyone. Golf has a code of conduct called "golf etiquette." It's designed for all golfers. When you watch the men and women touring professionals in a televised tournament, you'll notice that they are careful to observe golf etiquette. Since juniors are vastly outnumbered by adult golfers, it's important that you observe golf etiquette so that you'll be welcome on the golf course.

Here are simple rules of golf etiquette. Follow them, and other players will enjoy your company.

- Stand quietly and still as another golfer plays a shot.
- Stand out of the golfer's line of vision. Avoid standing directly behind the ball or behind the hole when a golfer is playing or preparing to play a shot.
- Make practice swings only when there's no chance that you'll disturb another golfer.
- Play quickly when it's your turn to play! This is very important. There's increasing concern about slow play and golfers who hold up others are unwelcome. Quickly walk to your ball and play your shot without delay.
- It's a good idea to let adults play through, but you should *always* let faster players play through, no matter what their

age. To invite golfers to play through, stand aside, where there's no chance that you'll be hit by an incoming ball, and wave them through. Stand quietly while they complete play and wait until they're well out of range before you resume play.

- If there's an open hole ahead of you, invite the group playing behind you to play through.
- If you're looking for a lost ball and a space opens in front of your group, invite the group behind to play through.
- Never hit into the group ahead! If you accidentally hit your ball into another group—perhaps you've hit your career-best tee shot and it goes farther than any you've ever hit before—

Stand quietly and still as another golfer plays a shot.

yell, "Fore!" as loudly as you can. Try to catch up to the group ahead. Explain and apologize, without interfering with their play.

• After playing from a bunker, rake and repair any damage.
• Never place your clubs in a bunker.
• Don't climb the high face of the bunker. Exit from the lower side or back.
• Avoid making divots with practice swings. If you make a divot with your swing or practice swing, replace it. Simply pick up the chunk of turf and gently press it back in place; it will grow back on its own.

Always yell, "Fore!" if your ball has a chance of striking another player.

Lay the flagstick carefully to the side of the green. A dropped flagstick can damage the putting surface.

- On the putting green, repair any mark made by the impact of your ball by pushing a tee into the ground along the circumference of the mark and gently pushing up the turf. Tamp down repaired turf with your putterhead.
- Don't stand or walk on the line of another golfer's putt.
- Never lay your golf bag on the green. Place it on the fringe or collar, on the side where you will exit the green.
- Carefully place the flagstick on the green or to the side of the green. A dropped or tossed flagstick damages the green.
- Before leaving the green, use your putterhead to tamp down any spike marks you've made, but only *after* all golfers in your group have holed out.
- If you find an extra club or any personal item on the golf course, return it to the golf shop so that it may be claimed.

- Leave the putting green as soon as everyone in your group has holed out. To avoid delaying play, mark your scorecard on the next tee, not while standing on the green.
- No horseplay and no displays of temper!
- Don't talk loudly or yell, unless you're shouting, "Fore!" You'll disturb golfers playing a nearby hole.
- Don't litter. Put trash in a trash can.
- "Please" and "thank you" are magic words on the golf course.

Observe these simple rules of etiquette and you'll be secure in knowing appropriate golf course conduct.

Learning the Ropes

While juniors are encouraged to play golf, they play at facilities designed for adults. This means they're expected to observe all the adult rules.

A little knowledge about the operation of a golf course will help you feel comfortable.

Where to Play

Public, municipal, and private courses are listed in the telephone book. Public courses are open to everyone. Municipal courses are usually open to everyone, but play is sometimes restricted to people who live in the city where the course is located. Private golf courses require that you be a member or the guest of a member in order to play.

If you want to play a nearby course, don't just show up. Telephone the course and ask to speak to someone in the golf shop. You'll want information about the cost of a round of golf. This is known as a "green fee." Some courses have lower green fees for junior players.

Most courses restrict the hours in which juniors are allowed to play. There are plenty of opportunities for junior golfers, but you may have to play only on weekdays, or in the late afternoon, and you may have to be accompanied by an adult. Be sure to ask if there are restrictions on junior golfers.

Tee Times

In order to play, you'll need to request a starting time or "tee time." This is an appointed time when you can tee off. If the course is a busy one, you may be required to play with at least three other golfers, so be prepared to organize your own group of players and bring them with you. Make the call several days in advance of when you want to play.

Your request for a starting time will go something like this:

You: "Hello, my name is John Smith. I'm a junior golfer and I'd like a tee time for Wednesday afternoon."

Professional: "We have a couple of openings. Do you have a foursome?" (A foursome is a group of four players, of which you are one.)

You: "Yes, I do."

Professional: "John, you can tee off Wednesday at 2:30 or at 4. Which do you want?"

You: "I'll take 2:30."

Professional: "Okay, who do you have?"

You: "I'm John Smith, and I have Billy Jones, Tim Brown, and Jack White."

Professional: "Alright—Smith, Jones, Brown, and White at 2:30. You're all set."

You: "Thank you very much."

At the Golf Course

When arriving to play or practice, check in at the golf shop, sometimes called the pro shop. The golf shop is usually connected to the larger clubhouse, but may be in a separate building. A sign will direct you, or feel free to ask directions.

The golf shop is run by the golf professional and his staff of assistant golf professionals. They stock a supply of golf clubs, golf balls, golf clothing, and equipment which they sell to golfers. Even if you have clubs and golf balls, there's a good chance you will eventually need to make a purchase. Perhaps you're low on golf tees, or need a Rule book. You can buy them here.

Rental sets of golf clubs are also available. A small fee gives you use of the clubs for a day, after which they must be returned to the shop. If you're renting clubs, you'll have to purchase your own golf balls, or bring balls with you.

Be sure to arrive at the course well ahead of your scheduled tee time. Give yourself at least 30 minutes in which to pay your green fee and perhaps hit a few practice putts before teeing off. If you plan to hit practice balls, you'll need even more time.

The Locker Room

Ask golf shop personnel for the location of the men's or women's locker room. Locker rooms include bathrooms, showers, benches to use while changing shoes, and lockers. The lockers can be rented for a monthly or yearly fee and are used to lock up personal items, such as clothing and shoes.

Many clubs, however, do not allow juniors in locker rooms unless accompanied by an adult. Be sure to ask.

Golf clubs are usually not allowed in locker rooms.

Golf Course Transportation

There are several ways to get around a golf course: walk and carry your golf bag, walk and pull your bag on a two-wheeled cart, ride in a motorized cart, or use a caddie to carry your clubs.

Most juniors walk and carry their own clubs. Motorized carts are expensive and you won't be permitted to rent one, or even drive one, until you have a driver's license.

Pull carts can be rented for a fee. Inquire in the golf shop. You may purchase your own from a golf shop, sporting goods store, or department store. Many courses, however, especially private courses, don't allow the use of pull carts.

Learn to carry your own clubs. Few juniors use caddies. Today, very, very few courses have caddies available. The miniscule number of courses with caddies are, in most cases, resort courses or private courses, and caddie fees are very expensive.

Practice

Most modern golf courses have practice areas: a driving range for hitting full shots, a practice putting green, and perhaps a practice chipping green and practice bunker. Inquire in the golf shop about practice facilities.

Staff members will direct you to practice areas and tell you how to rent practice balls. Some courses have ball-dispensing machines near the practice tee. These machines take either coins or tokens, which most often are purchased in the golf shop.

When practicing on a driving range, stay in the spaces between the tee markers. Stay behind the tee markers. If you hit a ball only a short distance, leave it. Never try to retrieve a practice ball. You can easily be hit by a ball struck by another player.

Practice balls must be left at the range or practice area. They belong to the club or golf professional. Practice balls are to be used only on the driving range. Never put practice balls in your golf bag. Never play a round of golf with practice balls.

Most courses allow the use of practice balls at the practice chipping green and practice bunker. When you've finished using these facilities, you may take the practice balls to the driving range. If practice balls were left by another player, don't retrieve them for use on the practice tee. Not only is it bad form, it's probably prohibited.

If you used the practice bunker, be sure to rake it with the rake provided for that purpose.

Use your own balls to practice putting. Choose a spot on the practice putting green which is removed from other players. After practicing, don't forget to retrieve your golf balls.

Teeing Off

Be on time for your starting time. If you're late, you've probably lost the opportunity to play on that particular day.

You may be required to check in in advance with a starter, a staff member who sees that golfers tee off in orderly fashion. If there is a starter, he'll be stationed in a small building near the first tee, or may simply stand near the tee. The starter has a list of all tee times.

You'll tee off on either the first or the tenth tee. If you're to tee off on the tenth tee, then you'll be playing the back nine before you play the front nine. On more crowded courses, this is a good way to move a number of golfers around the course. Check with the starter to find where you'll be teeing off.

If your tee time is, say, 2:30, you must be prepared to tee off at precisely 2:30. Have your club, tee, and ball in hand and be at the correct tee, ready to go.

If the course is extremely crowded or the weather is bad, tee times may be delayed. This means that you may have to wait as much as an hour, and tee off at 3:30, even if you have a 2:30 tee time. Be patient. Everyone else has been delayed by the conditions.

Playing the Course

Advice on golf course etiquette is included in lesson ten. Your most important responsibilities when playing are to be courteous, to play by the rules of golf, and to play quickly.

Golfers are newly concerned about slow play. With a growing number of golfers and a limited number of courses, everyone must play quickly in order to play at all. A round of golf for four people should take no more than four and a half hours, and that's a maximum!

Golfers who play too slowly will be warned to speed up by a "ranger." The ranger roves the golf course and has the duty of keeping play moving. The ranger can require golfers to let others play through and is to be obeyed. Golfers who play too slowly can also be asked to leave the golf course. Golfers who behave badly, by engaging in horseplay, being boisterous, or hitting a ball into another group of players, will also be asked to leave the course.

The ranger, golf professional, assistant professional, and starters have absolute authority over golfers.

The Golf Professional

The golf professional is there to help you learn the game through instruction. He or she is available for private lessons or group lessons, which are a bit less costly. If you'd like to take lessons, inquire in the golf shop about rates and available times.

The golf professional organizes events and tournaments, often puts together golfers with tee times, organizes everyday play, runs the junior and adult programs, and is an expert on the Rules of Golf.

Golf professionals are generally friendly folks who have made a career of promoting the game of golf and helping others learn to play the game well. They're happy to answer questions.

Assistant Golf Professionals

The golf professional usually has a staff of assistants who have also made a career of promoting the game.

The assistants work in the shop. They sell merchandise, take green fees, and often schedule tee times. They help the professional organize tournaments and are helpful on the rules of golf.

Assistant professionals are often available as instructors and to help run the junior program.

Handicaps

A handicap is one way of measuring your ability. It is a number applied to you as a golfer and measures the difference between par and your average score. If par for your course is 72, and your handicap is 20, then you generally shoot about 20 over par on your home course.

In adult competition, handicaps are used to provide a fair match between players of varying ability.

Juniors don't really need a handicap because handicaps aren't used in junior tournaments. In competition, juniors are grouped by age.

If you want to establish a handicap, however, inquire in the golf shop at your course and sign up. There's normally a fee. If you sign up to establish a handicap, you'll be required to turn in all future scorecards and each must be signed by another golfer with whom you played.

Part-time Jobs in Golf

Caddies have unfortunately been made obsolete in the United States by the widespread use of motorized golf carts. Only a relative handful of courses still employ caddies, so an age-old source of income for youngsters has virtually disappeared.

If you live near the largest golf resorts, such as Pinehurst, in North Carolina, or the Broadmoor Golf Club, in Colorado, you're near clubs that are among the last to use caddies. To find if you can take part, contact the head golf professional. Such golf courses have their own caddie training sessions.

There are, however, always odd jobs at golf courses. Volunteer to do odd jobs around the clubhouse, golf shop, or golf course. Youngsters who do such work generally get playing privileges at the course, access to golf equipment at a discount, and the professional will often help them with their golf games.

Junior Competition

When you've become a more advanced junior golfer, you may want to compete against other juniors. At most courses, juniors cannot play in adult tournaments. It's best to begin in junior tournaments at your own course or club. As you get better, you can then enter local, city, and regional tournaments.

Your course should have a bulletin board where golf events are posted. Consult this board to find out about scheduled junior tournaments. Regional, state, and national tournaments as well as local and club events are usually posted and entry blanks can be obtained in the golf shop.

Your golf professional and the junior program at your course will also help you. At my club, for example, we tell juniors who express an interest in tournaments about any upcoming events. We make sure they get entry blanks and know how to enter.

And our club has a junior golf team which plays against teams from other clubs.

Competing is less costly if several juniors from an area share expenses. Traditionally, three or four juniors get together for a car pool. This spreads the responsibility of transportation among several parents. And it's always nice to have friends with whom you can travel and play practice rounds.

For information on state, regional, and national junior tournaments, write to the United States Golf Association and request a junior tournament schedule. The USGA serves as a sort of clearinghouse for all junior events above the club level, and information includes addresses and entry fees for each tournament. Send your request to:

The United States Golf Association
Golf House
P.O. Box 708
Far Hills, NJ 07931–0708

Your Sample Scorecard

HOLE	1	2	3	4	5	6	7	8	9	OUT
YARDAGE										
PAR										
NOTES										

HOLE	10	11	12	13	14	15	16	17	18	IN
YARDAGE										
PAR										
NOTES										